PRINCIPLES OF
Effective Coaching

by
Allen Wade

Published by
REEDSWAIN INC

Library of Congress Cataloging - in - Publication Data

Wade, Allen
 Principles of Effective Coaching

ISBN No. 1-890946-12-5
Copyright © 1997 Allen Wade
Library of Congress Catalog Card Number 97-075735

Reedswain books are available at special discounts for bulk purchase. For details, contact the special Sales Manager at REEDSWAIN 1-800-331-5191.

Printed in the United States of America.

Credits: Art Direction, Layout, Design and Diagrams • Kimberly N. Bender
Cover Photo: EMPICS

REEDSWAIN BOOKS AND VIDEOS, INC.
612 Pughtown Road • Spring City Pennsylvania 19475
1-800-331-5191 • WWW.REEDSWAIN.COM

Table of Contents

Chapter 1
Coaching and Managing Soccer Players

1. Introduction

Most books on soccer coaching start with the techniques of the game. Some start, and end, by describing basic techniques and elementary tactical moves. Unfortunately teaching or coaching and learning aren't so simple.

Few authors mention players' or coaches' problems or their expectations of each other. Learning is treated as a simple matter of transfer of 'know how'. If only it was that easy; it isn't. Too many coaches are SOCCER coaches and negative soccer coaches at that. They tell players what not to do, usually after the event. They rarely tell players what to do and even more rarely why, where and when to do it. Only a few show players 'how', many claim unsubstantiated degrees of tactical wizardry; these are the touch line puppeteers, the game's string pullers.

> To be effective, coaches must gain access
> to the minds of players; it is not easy.

Most players, unfortunately, are expected to listen, learn and do!

The game doesn't so much need SOCCER coaches as PLAYER coaches.

PLAYER Coaches focus on players' needs and treat the players as they are not as they are assumed to be. Cross transference of understanding and skill development is a consequence of players understanding their deficiencies, identifying their needs and agreeing on a process of change. SOCCER COACHES assume that whatever knowledge of the game they have can be simply poured into the heads of players. Demonstrating a knowledge of the game may massage a coach's ego, it will do precious little for his players and even less for team success. The difference between PLAYER coaching and SOCCER coaching is important. If you are interested in improving as a PLAYER coach read on. If not you might be better off with someone else's book.

My book Soccer Teaching is exclusively concerned with soccer teaching and is complementary to this series although to imply that the four aspects of player preparation, coaching, teaching, managing and training are separate and unconnected would diminish the importance of each one. They are totally complementary and interdependent.

Chapter 2
Players' Needs and Expectations of a Coach.

W hat do players **WANT** from a coach when he is directing their activity in match play or on the practice and training grounds? Much more importantly, what do players **NEED** from a coach?

From observation and study a coach should be able to say what a player NEEDS in order to improve. What the player actually WANTS, however, may be rather different. Reconciling 'needs and wants' from a player's view point may be difficult but it is what coaching is all about. Success in coaching is based upon the clever and perceptive management of players; successful player management will be founded on a clear understanding of purpose and progress between all the parties involved. Soccer 'know-how' is important: the higher a coach's levels of involvement the greater the need for it but without a deep understanding of what makes players want to improve, the most comprehensive knowledge of the game may become hot air: a lot of it is.

Before examining the problems involved we need to define and clarify certain terms which are in common usage in soccer. These definitions are my own but will be understood by those teachers and coaches over whom, from time to time, I may have exerted some influence. Others may have different meanings for the same expressions of course; no doubt they will say so.

Coaching and teaching are highly complementary functions but they are not the same; the difference between the two is important. Teaching is concerned with improving an individual player's techniques together with his fundamental understanding of the game and its precepts or principles. A soccer teacher works with players entirely for their sake and not for any ulterior purpose such as team results. To a soccer teacher individual performance and development are everything even within the context of group interplay.

A soccer coach is concerned with team performance and success. Most of the work done by him is measured by the individual's performance and development in direct relation to improved team play. A coach may teach from time to time but his teaching will be aimed, ultimately, at team success.

A teacher should never be driven by match results, winning or losing; coaches always are. Both teaching and coaching, to be successful, involve skillful player management.

It is vital in any learning situation that learner and coach (or teacher) use the same language. New words and expressions must be carefully explained to players, even to senior players. Jargon or buzz words are often used to give, falsely, an impression of coach superiority; the players' response may be to give an equally false impression of stupidity. Players and coaches must have a relationship which enables them to ask each other what they mean if there is a block to understanding.

> Ignorance arises not out of a lack of understanding,
> it arises out of an unwillingness to seek it.

By all means use special words to add meaning and 'colour' to coaching; coaching is, before all else, an inspirational function, but take the trouble to say what you mean.

From time to time a coach will see the need to teach one or more players new techniques, techniques without which a player, even a mature, international player, and even more importantly his team, may be seriously handicapped. The most obvious example is where a player is limited to using one foot. Whatever the need, a coach will have to take the player back into very elementary learning situations. Increasing the range of a player's technical skills (techniques), on the other hand, is fundamental to a soccer teacher's role: that is what he or she should be about. A coach teaches to increase team capabilities and thereby improve their results. He will rarely if ever teach to improve the full range of a player's techniques, he simply hasn't got the time.

Techniques, orthodox and unorthodox, are the bedrock of high class soccer skill; teaching them is harder than it may seem.

Skill is unlikely to be acquired in unrealistic situations, in repetitive 'drills' for example or in circus style ball juggling. Drills may have a place in soccer training but the return in skill gained from the investment of time in drill practice or in 'solo juggling' isn't really worth the players' effort, or the coach's.

CONTROLLED OPPOSITION in practice and **LOADED** (conditioned) GROUP PLAY are vital elements in the design of effective skill learning and practice situations. We shall examine both in detail later.

Over-exposure to **UNCONTROLLED OPPOSITION**, as in league or knock-out match play, at early stages of development can be entirely destructive, except where the player himself chooses the level of opposition. Players are smart, they seldom choose levels of opposition or competition with which they are unable to cope: quite the opposite in fact.

Match play alone will not induce higher levels of skill. Excessive championship match play inhibits players; results, inevitably, become more important than individual development; players play to win before they know how to play! "Kick and hope football becomes ingrained: it is impossible to eradicate."

What do players specifically expect from their coaches?
2.1 They want and need to know what exactly the coach's personal and profession-

al standards and ideals are. They particularly want explicit confirmation of how he wants the game to be played: in other words they need to understand and appreciate his sense of style. It will be of little use asking players to play 'good soccer' unless the coach sets out in detail exactly what his idea of good soccer is.

2.2 Ideals are important as reference points but team results are matters of realism. Players want to know how the coach intends to set about improving team results and changing performances where necessary, and in that order.

2.3 Players are quick to sense conflict between 'those in charge', the coaches, and themselves or their team mates. Coaches will deserve merit when they ascertain and take note of the players' views of their team's condition and its problems. Soccer is a matter of cause and effect but players tend to be more interested in effects than causes

2.4 A coach is expected to produce simple, reasonable solutions to all problems. His predecessor, in desperation, probably sought all kinds of answers, simple and complex. Solving team play problems in soccer isn't merely a matter of technical or tactical expertise, it's a matter of confidence; the confidence which a coach has in his own perceptions of the game and the confidence which the players are persuaded to have in the coach's judgment and decision making.

2.5 Players expect the coach to get the best out of them. They may not be sure how this can be achieved or what it actually is but they expect a coach to see performances, especially 'problem' performances, from their points of view as much as from his own. Coaches are expected to identify individual and collective problems posed by opponents, immediately, and come up with solutions, sooner if possible! Players want to be told precisely what to do to put matters right. Imprecise, extravagantly expressed tactical exhortations which are barely relevant are likely to be scornfully dismissed, sooner or later, and eventually the coach along with them. If a coach can't come up with answers it will pay him to come clean and say so before calling upon all the team's resources for assistance.

This is known as sharing responsibility; it is important.

2.6 Most players enjoy being led positively, even firmly; some have no wish to be led at all. Replace them, quickly. A coach will be expected to tell players specifically what to do to 'put things right' whether they are technical details of performance or tactical moves.

> Players are not keen to be told what they did wrong;
> they much prefer to hear how to do it right.

2.7 Coaches are expected to make coaching and practice interesting, occasionally exciting and above all profitable; training on the other hand must be seen by players to be relevant and endurable, just!

The process of player development within successful team play must be the result of consultation, agreement and planning.

2.8 Players have personal as well as professional problems; the former frequently give rise to the latter. Coaches are expected to be aware of all player problems and to be miraculous when necessary in solving them.

2.9 Players expect fairness in all their dealings with coaches. Players may transgress over agreed matters of attitude and behavior; they may behave unfairly to each other and to their coaches. This can never justify retaliatory behavior.

2.10 Players expect coaches to lift (inspire) them when necessary: it often is. Playing sport, especially team sport, can be a matter of moods. Players may persuade themselves that everything is against them and that losing is inexplicable but inevitable. The coach must deal with this apparently intractable problem when he himself may be only marginally less depressed. The difference is that coaches are not allowed the luxury of depression.

Players expect their coaches to be totally and predictably consistent in their attitudes and behavior.

2.11 We all need and seek peer approval. Players need recognition for what they are and what they try to achieve not only from the coach but even more so from their team mates. This has to be done scrupulously, fairly, and seriously. Jokers within the team will try to reduce performance assessment, especially the assessment of practice performance, to the comical. Usually this is because the jokers themselves, aware of defects in their own performances, don't want the spotlight of assessment to be focused on them.

Jokers are a problem; they are attention seekers, anyone's attention will do. They are best treated in isolation from the rest of the team, seriously but firmly.

Any soccer coach who sets out to meet the above player expectations is well prepared for profitable player relationships.

Chapter 3
The Coach: His Needs.

A professionally well trained coach will need expertise in the following subject areas.

Human Growth and Maturation.
The Psychology of Teaching and Learning
Man-Management
Human Kinetics
The Development of Individual, Group and Team Skills
The Principles of Attack and Defense
The Development of Strategies and Tactics and Match Analysis
The Laws of The Game and Ethical Behavior
The Theory and Practice of Exercise and Training
The Treatment and Rehabilitation of Injured Players
Practice Design
Planning and Preparing Practice and Training Programs

Some of the countries which sought my advice in obtaining the services of highly expensive coaches would have been far better off investing in soccer teachers. Certainly that was true of the United States of America; it may still be. In America the sports coach enjoys enormous credibility and fame: more so than in Britain although times are changing, albeit slowly. A coach is concerned with refining and developing individual and team performance to meet the demands of match play; match play is synonymous with results which are the criteria by which a coach will be judged. Soccer is a game for open minds; without imaginative coaches, players and teams are unlikely to make progress. Similarly a coach should reasonably expect open mindedness from his players. Both are in the trial and success business but success usually involves change. Without open minded players change will be difficult. Fundamental to mutually beneficent open mindedness is the regular interchange of open and honest appraisals. A coach is expected to say what he thinks, honestly and fairly, about team and individual performances in match play and in practice. Players must be encouraged to be as honest and open in their perceptions of the coach's coaching and training methods. Both players and coaches need to know how and to what extent each contributes to improvement. In these circumstances even the most uncooperative players can be transformed instantly . . . well, almost.

A frequent and fair examination of practice and 'in game' improvements is absolutely fundamental to coaching success.
Mark these words carefully.

A soccer season is a test of both mental and physical endurance. A coach will decide on the pace and intensity of practice and training according to perceived need at any particular time. Some will be conducted at reduced levels of intensity, especially where the group is changing its work pattern or emphasis. Similarly the coach will see the need for higher levels of work intensity from time to time according to results and to the changing demands of the match program. When he requires maximum effort in certain areas of work he has the right to expect the players to give it without question. If there is a need for explanation, that will be in order, but occasionally the coach will sense a need for which he is unable to give explanation until the work has been completed.

All practice and training should be enjoyable, understandable and objective but from time to time it has to be very demanding. The coach is expected to make those decisions.

Chapter 4
The Work of a Coach.

A coach's job description will include the following, **He should:**

4.1 Select and prepare players for competitive match play.

4.2 Plan, direct and personally supervise practice and training routines, short, medium and long term, to ensure the players' optimum effectiveness during competition and during their playing careers with that particular team. Head coaches have a fundamental responsibility to be in personal charge of player preparation. They may delegate certain areas of work to assistants from time to time but the reins will always be in their hands.

4.3 Educate players in the fundamentals of strategical and tactical play.

A sensible aim for all coaches is to prepare players to be able to adjust play tactically as if the team had no coaches.

One of the best English coaches in my experience would occasionally start a practice session himself, set the objectives and leave his players to coach themselves. He would disappear and return maybe ninety minutes later.

4.4 Set out, review and change, where necessary, a team's strategical aims and tactical objectives before, during and after matches.

Communication between the coach and his players during match play is very important, occasionally vital. All players, especially the key players, need to know precisely how communication will take place. They must learn whatever bench signals may be used and they must practice the transmission of messages as in match play. Certain key players, the team captain and one or two player leaders must be taken into the confidence of the coach and virtually undertake apprenticeships in tactical coaching.

4.5 Evaluate a team's playing resources (the individual players) and make the necessary adjustments in the light of current or intended team performance.

4.6 Direct the coaching, practice and training of supplementary teams, particularly those involved in the development of junior players. It is of incalculable importance to junior players that the top coach is constantly and personally monitoring their progress.

4.7 Consult closely with the medical and para medical staff on player fitness in general and particularly on post injury, rehabilitative fitness.

A professional coach once told me that in his opinion, when players were recovering from serious injuries they were, in a way, mentally ill. They were worried about the possibility of never recovering; they were deeply concerned about regaining their team place; if they had wives and families they were anxious about the long term prospects for employment; they felt useless and completely out of things.

A head coach must make time to assume an active and regular role in a player's rehabilitation.

4.8 Represent the players' best interests within the stated aims and objectives of general club administration.

In professional soccer in England a manager or head coach is often regarded as part of the business management side of the club's affairs, or he assumes that he is! While he should have final say on player movements in and out of the club, in every other sense his interests are the players' interests and he should be prepared to fight for them where they are fair and equitable. A minority of professionals can be greedy and will conjure up unreasonable demands. The majority are sensible people and will appreciate reasonable management decisions. The coach should make sure that fairness and reasonableness prevail. Some managers try to run with the foxes and hunt with the hounds; they are quickly found out.

Players are extremely good at finding out about things of which they should have no knowledge.

Greedy and persistently dissatisfied players should be moved out as soon as convenient; they are never worth the trouble involved in trying to meet their insatiable demands.

The role of the coach, in British soccer, is no more than fifty years old. British professional teams, traditionally, have been 'managed' rather than coached; they still are, to the obvious detriment of the national game. In England a coach has usually been seen to hold an inferior position to that of a manager and a soccer teacher's position is considered inferior to that of the coach. Nothing wrong with that if all managers were experienced and well trained coaches and if all coaches had received serious professional training and served their time as teachers. In England anyone can become a paid coach or manager, even my 92 year old mother! And some clubs, having 'gone through' half a dozen managers or coaches in as many years, could do a lot worse! Many soccer managers in England, perhaps most, are appointed almost solely on their reputations as former players; annual manager mortality rates are upwards of thirty percent! Need more be said?

A British manager may have little if any skill or experience and even less training in organizing, planning and directing practice and training. His tactical knowledge may be more illusory than real yet, because of 'fame and name' he may have absolute control of all matters affecting a club's players from the full professionals down to the youngest schoolboy associates. Many even negotiate player trading deals but the less said about those the better.

Little wonder that the financial status of the majority of professional soccer clubs in England is precarious. The position of manager is an anachronism other than where his job description is explicit. This is the situation throughout mainland Europe, Britain excepted. After all, what can a team manager do that a first class coach can't?

For the sake of clarity let's take a brief look at another person involved in the player preparation and development business. Outside Britain, the trainer enjoys similar status to the American coach and fulfills the same role. He picks the team; he directs the players in training and in match play; in collaboration with expert medical back-up he monitors the treatment and rehabilitation programs of injured players.

In Britain, a trainer traditionally combined the athletic and gymnastic preparation of players with the elementary (I use the word advisedly) treatment of injuries. In recent years, as a highly trained physical therapist, he has been concerned exclusively with the treatment and rehabilitation of injured players with, in some cases, a sort of advisory role in general physical conditioning. The latter because so few coaches and almost no managers have adequate backgrounds in the anatomy and physiology of exercise and training. A trainer, in the British sense, needs the knowledge and experience of a specialized medical auxiliary.

He needs a considerable understanding of:

Human kinetics and soccer movement.

Anatomy and physiology of exercise and training

Treatment and rehabilitation of injuries.

Advanced medical aid.

The psychology of motivation.

It is important in any organization that, whatever their titles, each of the people in it knows precisely what his (or her) responsibilities are and to whom they are answerable. They must have clearly defined areas of responsibility and authority; vagueness leads to ineffectiveness.

Responsibility without authority leads to indecision, to 'empire building' and to interpersonal rivalry.

The sum total of all that is inefficiency. The sufferers are the players and ultimately the clubs.

4.9 Coach selection: A Profile For Success.

Professional players, however celebrated, cannot simply 'pick up' the expertise needed to coach. Playing the game at the highest level has nothing to do with coaching ability or potential. Former players, untrained in coaching, merely regurgitate what was done to them by their own managers and coaches, understanding little if any of it. Worse, they are often allowed to appoint assistants with significantly more inadequacies than their own. Usually these are members of the 'old comrades' associations which prevail in professional soccer. This results in the gross ill-treatment of players.

A nation's best players deserve high class, professionally trained and highly qualified coaches.

Germany, second to none in world soccer, insists on high level qualification, by examination, for all professional coaches. The policy has paid handsome dividends. All the 'advanced' European countries, Holland, Italy, Denmark, Norway, Sweden, and so on, require 'top' coaches to gain appropriate qualifications after serious study and stringent examinations. In what was socialist Eastern Europe, training and qualification for soccer coaches were conducted at university degree levels.

The moral for all developing soccer countries must be, beware the coaching 'pretenders', wherever they come from. Listening to them is only marginally less expensive than hiring them.

4.91 The Successful Coach's Principal Attributes.

All coaches will be different; their perceptions of some aspects of the game will differ. They will have different personalities but in all the respects that matter they will exhibit great similarities. The following are those attributes upon which I place importance in their order of importance to me. You may differ but I would be surprised if you didn't include most of these attributes in judging your coaches' personal qualities.

(a) LEADERSHIP AND INTELLIGENCE.

Some may regard these qualities as separate; in my view they are complementary. Without applied intelligence, leadership deteriorates into exhortation or deviousness. Looking into the minds of players perceptively requires intelligence of a high order. Coaches have to persuade, cajole and occasionally compel their players to go along with them. I am of course talking about Head Coaches, those whose heads are always on the block. They must be prepared to lead and to accept the responsibility which goes with the authority and expectations of anyone in the top position.

(b) ANALYTICAL ABILITY.

The ability to 'read' a game of soccer is vital. Coaches must become students of the game and they are likely to learn infinitely more while teaching and coaching than they ever learned as players. Coaches need to be expert movement analyzers as well as tactical analysts.

(c) CONFIDENCE AND DECISIVENESS.

Players want answers to their problems 'now', preferably sooner; they sense indecision or 'waffle' a mile away. High importance is given to decisiveness and confidence because players know from personal experience how important they are.

(d) INTEGRITY AND RELIABILITY.

Even dishonest players value honesty in their coach, and they absolutely demand reliability. They will even accept open criticism within the team as long as it is the same for everyone and so long as it is phrased constructively. Coaches become recipients of many personal secrets or confidences; their players must be totally certain of the coach's reliability in protecting those confidences.

(e) ENTHUSIASM.

The coach has to sustain his enthusiasm and that of everyone else often under the most trying circumstances, and he is expected to! Players are often mentally 'up and down' other than where a team is on a 'big roll' of success. Then the need is for the coach to control enthusiasm and prevent overconfidence occurring. A coach who is other than consistently enthusiastic, whatever the team's results or mood, is in the wrong job.

(f) VISION AND IMAGINATION.

In professional soccer, training and practice can become boring: it shouldn't but it can. The English season for professionals is the ultimate test of everyone's enthusiasm and thereby of the coach's imagination in keeping boredom at bay.
Practice schedules have to be altered and patterns changed without affecting results, other than for the better of course. That's why 'big name', untrained coaches and managers fail. Their lack of insight into and training for the whole business of player preparation precludes any possibility of imaginatively changed routines.

(g) COPING WITH UNPLEASANTNESS.

There are many circumstances which are or become unpleasant in soccer. Players are injured, sometimes seriously: recovery is arduous: a player can never be sure of regaining his place in the team. Older players, coming to the ends of their careers have to be moved on or out: it is a painful process. Players have to be dropped for loss of form and loss of form can arise out of many causes, not all to do with soccer. A coach has to take all these problems on board and deal with them sensitively and to everyone's satisfaction. Players not directly concerned with a situation will watch critically how the coach deals with it. Soccer players are inquisitive animals and display intense interest in matters which don't concern them; it goes with the game.

(h) ORGANIZATION AND ADMINISTRATION.

Professional soccer players are the most disorganized people I have ever met; their wives are exactly the opposite: they have to be! Time keeping? What **IS** time? Tidiness? Have you ever seen a bombstruck bed room? And of course they demand impeccable organization from their coaches. Woe betide a coach who schedules a meeting for 2 o'clock and doesn't appear until ten minutes later.

In practice everything must go as clockwork, or else.

A professional coach must leave absolutely nothing to chance; every contingency has to be covered.

Those are the main attributes I would look for in a coach. There may be others but those provide a foundation upon which selection for training and appointment as a coach at the higher levels of the game would be based.

4.92 Preparing the Ground.

Having selected potentially talented coaches carefully, a similar degree of care must be given to the thoroughness of their education. In some countries, coach education has been placed, exclusively, in the hands of academic physical educators and sports scientists; most of those countries came to regret the decision. Coaching isn't an academic process it is a practical skill but there are areas of expertise needed which can be drawn from the specialist subject areas listed in 3 previously. Effective coach training courses must ensure that all subjects in the curricula are directly related to the performances of players and to the practical needs of players and coaches.

Relating the different subject areas to the game and to the preparation of players is best done by specialists who themselves have significant experience as practical coaches albeit not necessarily at the highest levels of play. Acquiring practical coaching expertise and experience is best done in the regular company of outstandingly successful coaches much like the in service training and experience gained by young doctors.

The process by which effective coaching is planned and executed will be based upon the following.

    (a) Agreement that change (improvement) is needed.

    (b) Identification of the changes needed to bring about player and team
       improvement.

    (c) Exposure and elimination of whatever obstacles to change can be identified.

    (d) Agreement on the processes by which change will be effected.

    (e) Setting out a 'map of change' and seeking agreement from all concerned
       about the 'markers' by which progress, or otherwise, will be assessed.

    (f) Laying down an agreed time scale for reviewing the progress made.

This may not go down too well with those coaches who begin and end their work with "Now hear this!"

Performances improve when players accept the need to learn new skills and to polish those already learned. Improving personal (technical) and combined (tactical) performance depends upon players' and coaches' commitments to high levels of practice, in duration and intensity. There is no easy path to high skill. The person at the center of these developments, the coach, must listen to and understand all points of view and use that understanding to accelerate improvement in performance. He will do this by showing players how and when to train and to practice, in the game and outside it. He will have a clear idea of where the journey of development may

15 lead: how far that journey is: what obstacles are likely to be encountered on the way and to what extent each player is or can be equipped, mentally and physically, to deal with those obstacles.

Chapter 5
The Coaching Business

5.1 Coach and Player Meetings: Maximizing Impact.

Face to face meetings between players and a coach directly affect player performance and subsequent working relationships. If they don't, don't have them!

Meetings can result in mutual appreciation or they can be disasters: clearly they are worth thinking about. Personal relationships depend heavily on initial impact. Impact determines the extent to which each finds the other worth looking at, worth listening to, worth speculating about and the range of expectations each has of the other. In the case of a soccer coach meeting a group of players for the first time, a 'player perception' of the coach is likely to have gone before him. In professional soccer these perceptions will have been shaped by the coach's public reputation (real or imagined), the results achieved by the teams with which he has worked, by his style and, at the top, by media portrayals. Additionally, his new players will have sought the opinions of other players and anyone else with whom the coach formerly worked. Some of these perceptions may be accurate, others may be distorted, a few may be malicious: all are likely to be magnified versions of the real thing and all may change on the basis of the first meeting. It is in the coach's interests that the change is for the better: it will pay him to prepare carefully.

Preparation will be based on the coach's perceptions of the team which he is taking over. Often he will know a good deal about the players. He will have tried to assess 'the state of mind' of the club. He will have evaluated the 'management atmosphere' established by his predecessor. He should know of 'problem' players and players' problems, real or imagined. Now he has to 'eye ball' the players: to meet them face to face.

5.11 Organization and Location.

The atmosphere should be semi-formal; players seated so that each can see and be seen. This is a professional meeting. The coach needs eye-to-eye contact with each player whenever he chooses. Making personal contact with people who hear but cannot see or be seen, or don't want to be, is a quick way of losing impact.

If audio or other practical 'props' are needed the coach himself must make sure that they are available and working; depending on others before real authority is established is too chancy. 'Stage managing' has to be done by the coach; it pays to be certain. Successful coaches are good organizers; getting the little things right immediately will impress.

'Pro' soccer players are among the worst organized people I have ever met. That's why they choose well organized wives! However, they are changeable, the players that is, but only by example.

One of England's team managers insisted on a complete remodeling of the team's cavernous changing rooms in Wembley Stadium, a room which could have easily accommodated both teams and the marching band! From his vantage point in the reshaped and seriously reduced room he needed eye to eye contact with each player, whatever that player happened to be doing. Many American stadiums have open fronted individual changing cubicles. Each player is secluded from team mates but always within eye contact of the coach. The facility for 'eye balling' players is important to coaches who need to make important tactical points when time to do so is very limited.

5.12 Timing and Scheduling.

Everyone needed at a meeting should be able to attend at the time stated; one player will seek permission to be excused; don't give it, he is trying it on! Offer to re-schedule the meeting and tell the others; miraculously he will be available.

Soccer players are best kept off balance all the time! Never allow your players to know exactly where they stand with you. It may worry them but it will stop them worrying you!

All meetings should begin precisely at the time stated irrespective of who may be delayed or missing. There will be at least one late comer, probably the one who tried to get out of the meeting in the first place; he is a trier, welcome him ultra-politely and ask him to see you later; make sure that it is much later. He will definitely not enjoy the rest of the meeting but he will not be late again! Timekeeping is a matter of personal discipline and that is a high priority management objective. Certain considerations may be open to negotiation between coach and players, punctuality isn't one of them.

5.13 Participants.

If the meeting includes club officials, who speaks, about what and for how long must be cleared beforehand; a tight time-table must be adhered to. Players are easily bored; bored players are quick to find other interests to occupy their minds, not all of which are socially acceptable.

The meeting objectives (agenda) must be clearly set out, otherwise players are likely to be unreceptive, certainly at subsequent meetings. Whenever the business moves to playing (and players') problems it must be private and exclusive: players and coaching staff only.

5.2 Establishing Authority.

Assume that all players 'try things on' with anyone in authority, most will. They have a fascination with finding out how far they can exceed any restrictions or dodge any obligations. Childish it may be but it is built into their competitive and sometimes immature natures. Never give players an inch! And make sure punishment fits the crime, plus five percent! Very few people, soccer players included, are really difficult to manage. But, like runaway horses, they have to be kept on very tight reins and pulled up short occasionally, sometimes painfully.

Coaches have to make an early choice about familiarity. There really is no choice; familiarity destroys authority and is contrary to my 'off balance' principle established earlier. The success of any collaborative action depends upon the willingness of everyone involved to stick to agreed procedures: in soccer, both on and off the field. Those straying off line, willfully, must be 'redirected' decisively for the good of everyone.

There are coaches who think that authority goes with the territory; they are wrong. A coach may have power but not a shred of authority. Authority in coaching is based upon mutual respect. The coach respects his players for what they are and they learn to respect him for what he stands for: provided always that he makes what he stands for crystal clear.

Power without genuine authority is a form of dictatorship. Of course in professional soccer coaching dictators have always existed but not for long. A coach earns authority by establishing respect for his ideals in all aspects of life, personal and professional.

5.21 Discipline.

Discipline is best maintained where subordinates are never quite certain what the reaction of a superior to unacceptable behavior or performance will be. Players should know what agreed levels of punishment for different transgressions or offenses are but they should never know what the coach's application of his punishment options are likely to be. Effective disciplinarians are good actors; they produce totally convincing albeit changeable 'faces' to meet differing situations. Punishment (and discipline) is in the mind: it may have different consequences but must be intimidating if it is to deter.

If punishment fails to deter players from repeating unacceptable actions it is a waste of time.

It is successful when it deters would be transgressors, thereby causing behavior to change significantly; the rest is pure theatre! Allowing emotions to govern behavior in a disciplinary situation is a contradiction in terms. Emotion produces uncontrolled behavior and discipline is best effected by controlled, considered action. Disciplinary skills, like all skills, can be taught, learned and improved through practice. It is impossible to switch from easy familiarity to a stern, critical, remonstrative attitude without practice; it is also not desirable, until the coach is in total control of any foreseeable consequences.

Players are required to practice their playing skills and coaches must practice their management skills.

Occasionally coaches have to take unpleasant action: the sooner it is done the better. The greater the delay, the more painful the experience will be, for the coach!

Coaches must keep players at a distance. High standards of behavior and commitment should be set and demanded unremittingly, especially in the early stages of a working relationship.

Discipline should be exercised as soon as it becomes necessary; delaying until action is overwhelmingly necessary makes life difficult. By then, often, the situation has reached crisis level. It is a requirement of a coach's managerial skill to anticipate crises and prevent them happening. A crisis implies failure on the part of the coach to take curative action in time. In business, this is called fire fighting. The best way of fighting fires, as an Irish friend told me, is to put them out before they start.

Meetings between a coach and a player, involving the discussion of personal matters, misbehavior, criticism of playing performance, attitude to training or to other players, are best conducted on a one-to-one or two-to-one basis where the 'two' are the coach and an assistant. In the latter case, the senior coach must prepare his assistant for the meeting. He must outline his expectations of the meeting and of his assistant's participation. The coach conducts the meeting and the assistant contributes only at direct invitation. They use each other to achieve their objectives.

Coaches in disagreement are 'easy meat' for difficult players; 'vibes' of disharmony are seized on with uncanny perception. Some players are expert manipulators, watch out for them! If there is any manipulating to be done, the coach should do it!

5.3 Coaching by Objectives.

The coach's initial meeting with his players and all subsequent meetings must have specific objectives. Calling a meeting without clear objectives is inviting trouble. Ask yourself if a meeting is really necessary or whether it just seems like a good idea. If it just seems like a good idea, it probably isn't! Initially, the coach has his own objectives but at the same time he will try to anticipate or discover what the players expect of him; coaching and management are two way processes. The following are some examples of objectives which, for an initial meeting, a coach may find relevant.

(a) To define, unequivocally, the coach's beliefs about the way the game should be played.

Until the coach is prepared to say how he will judge a team's overall performance the players will be unsure of him and of themselves. Changes in strategy and basic tactics may become necessary for all kinds of reasons: injuries to key players: the team losing form and confidence: a series of matches against better teams: poor results: special matches e.g. knock out competitions during a league season and so on. A good coach will anticipate and make such preparation as he can for all contingencies as part of medium and longer term preparation. Many coaches spend their working lives trying to coach 'good soccer' without ever telling players what it is!

Only after ten years as national coaching director in England, often using the expression 'good football (soccer)', did I realize that many of the coaches in front of me didn't really know what I meant. All had been successful professionals, many were international players but any assumption that we were all speaking the same language was a great mistake, mine! And they weren't about to admit to not knowing; not when my staff and I would eventually decide who had passed the course and who hadn't! Score in management communication? Zero out of ten!

   (b) To set out his expectations of the players in their attitudes towards competition: in their attitudes towards training and practice and not least in their personal conduct and appearance.

A coach will be unwise always to lay down absolute rules, but all requirements should be attainable and enforceable. A coach who says what will happen and fails to ensure that it does is well on the way to having serious management problems. Never is a word which I never use!! But a coach should **NEVER** say what he will do and then fail to do it.

Nevertheless before expectations are firmly established a coach needs to weigh up very carefully the situation which he has inherited. He also needs an intimate knowledge of the make up and background of each player under his direction. Change will be necessary and expected but unreasonable change initiated immediately may sow the seeds of reaction.

   (c) To describe in broad terms the route towards progress which he sees the team taking and how he, and they, will measure that progress.

All attainment targets should be reachable and therefore, initially at least, they should be modest. If he is smart, the coach may insinuate (but not state) that maybe the players aren't good enough to reach the targets but that together he and they may be able to transform the situation. There are few better motivational devices in sport than to suggest, in all seriousness of course, that an athlete may have difficulty in attaining what is clearly a modest target.

Short term targets **MUST** be achievable: nothing breeds confidence like success.

Where a team has suffered long term failure, targets need to involve elementary precepts (principles) which, as soon as possible, are translatable into the needs of each individual player. During periods of failure, and they will happen, players need immediate 'psychological first aid' to stop the hemorrhage of confidence. They need to know specifically, very specifically, what to do to improve effectiveness.

Setting and adjusting team, group and individual achievement targets is a vital management skill. All objectives (achievement targets) should be measurable. Where those objectives involve soccer skill, improvement may be a matter of opinion. For example, a wide back may be poor at clearing the ball when facing his own goal. This may involve the technique of kicking on the turn or even over head. It is one thing to improve this technique in simple straight forward practice situations it is quite another, unfortunately, to reproduce the technique in the pressure of an important competitive match. In these circumstances it is vital that the player and the coach discuss and agree **WHERE** the player's skill level is at the beginning of the rehabilitation process and **HOW** progress will be measured at various stages. However expert the coach, the player is the only person really able to judge the extent to which skill improvement has taken place. Skill measurement (assessment) should be recorded, however subjective those measurements may seem to be.

Whatever needs to be altered in performance must be a matter of record. Without records the needs for and the extent of change don't really exist.

Coaches and players need to know absolutely where they stand, where they are going and the extent to which they are getting there. Many players and some coaches, bad ones that is, prefer to exist in a world of unregistered opinion. They hope that without measurement and records they are beyond judgment: maybe they are but their results aren't!

5.31 Planning and Preparation.

Coaching and training (and teaching) are either progressive and measurable or they are merely hopeful. Effective planning for a season's match program should commence with the end of the forthcoming season rather than as most people think at the beginning.

5.32 Seasonal.

Assuming that a team hopes to win the league or the knock out competition in which it plays or even to improve significantly on a previous season's performance, success or otherwise will be governed by that team's ability to maintain relevant levels (I hesitate to use the word 'peak') of form and fitness to the very last match. That will be possible only where the whole season's planning and preparation, from beginning to end, is set up and adjusted on that premise. Any team which suddenly finds itself needing higher levels of capability, whether to win things or to avoid losing, will find the increase in preparation intensity difficult to accommodate. A team whose preparation has been planned at a high level of intensity can, if necessary, ease down occasionally, perhaps to accommodate unforeseen stress in a long and demanding competition, without causing a drop in form. Poorly trained coaches in professional soccer have been known to step up preparation for the four or five days immediately before a special match in the fond but mistaken belief that fitness and form will have been improved as a consequence. And so it may have been but not for a match four or five days away. Human adaptation to changes in preparation routines isn't achieved as readily as that.

So called 'special' training in English football, founded more upon myth than upon proven method, has been a joke for a century or more. It arises out of a failure to understand the basic neuro-physiological principles of sports preparation.

5.33 Preparation Cycles.

Where the playing season is very long, as in England, preparation should be based upon cycles of four or five weeks so that a forty week playing season becomes eight five week cycles or ten of four weeks.

In diagram 1, I am assuming a preparation cycle of four weeks. Three weeks of build up to a 100% intensity level of training and practice input followed by one week of relatively low input and at the end of that week an important match. All matches are important but some are more important than others and often for a variety of reasons.

Each cycle will start with the players at an assumed practice and training level of 100%. This is the perceived, ideal level of readiness for a very important match or series of matches. It is the level which should be the ultimate aim of pre-season preparation. Immediately following the end of one cycle, preparation intensity in the following unit will be adjusted to the 75% level approximately. That is to say the last week of one cycle and the first day or two of a subsequent cycle will be at relatively low levels of intensity.

Over the following three weeks that level of intensity will be re-developed to the 100% level but in the last week of the cycle, week four, preparation again will be almost exclusively mental and methodical involving low levels of work intensity.

We may call this 'the rhythm method' since seasonal preparation follows a wave like pattern. The only adjustments which will be made will be those caused by injuries, extreme weather and playing conditions and very important matches. If very important matches can be foreseen then the peak week of preparation should end approximately five days before that particular match irrespective of the overall length of the cycle.

Cyclical adjustments will have to be made to cater for ongoing knock out competitions where participation cannot be entirely foreseen: better to assume that it will happen rather than not. The four week cycle may have to be extended to five weeks, on a four to one ratio of intense to not so intense work. Lengthening the cycle will be better than reducing it to three weeks say ie. a two to one ratio of demanding to less severe work.

Some coaches within my experience consider away matches to be significantly more demanding than those at home. Consequently they devise mini cycles within the basic cycle so that peak targets are hit in the beginning of the week at the end of which an 'away' match is scheduled. Home matches are treated as ordinary fitness and form development parts of the cycle.

It is not widely realized in professional soccer that change, ie. the effects of sustained coaching, practice and training, is significantly enhanced by rhythmical methods in which neuro-physiological 'systems' have time to adjust to the effects of change. It is also not widely appreciated that in any situation in which the system has to adapt to change through training, tuition and practice, the process of change continues for a short time after all training, tuition and practice has ceased. A kind of learning momentum is developed which extends beyond actual involvement in the process. It is very important that coaches understand this and incorporate it in the design of preparation cycles. Any beliefs that training or practice effects are immediately absorbed and available for use have more basis in witch doctory than in fact. And there's a lot of witch doctory about in soccer coaching and practice.

A Four Week Preparation Cycle

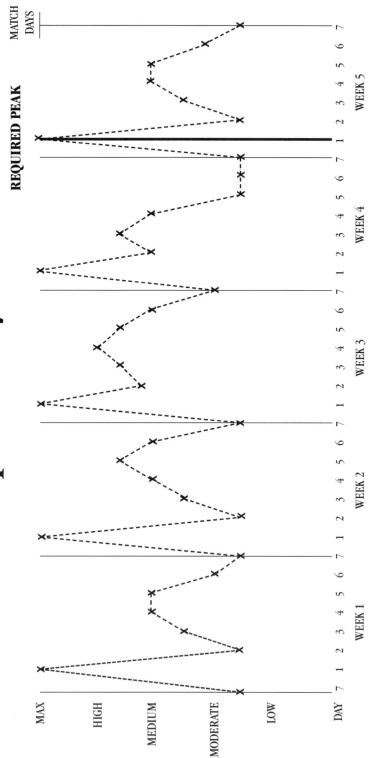

Diagram 1

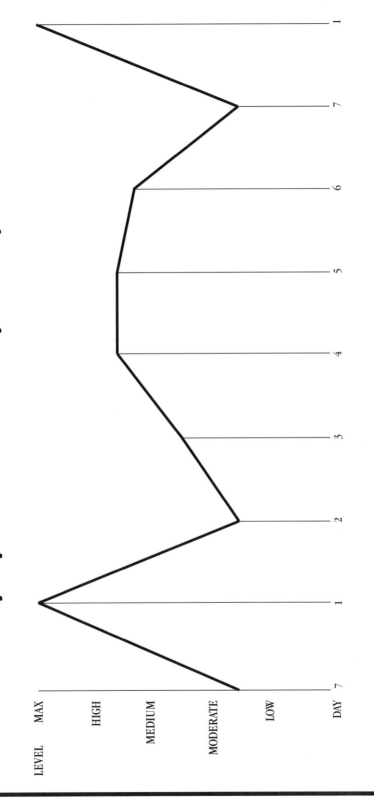

Weekly Cycle - Match Day is Day 1

Diagram 2

5.34 The Preparation Week diagram 2.

Within a four week cycle each week's work will also follow a wave like pattern.

The week-end match day, Saturday or Sunday, is counted as **day 1**, and is regarded as a commitment of maximum intensity.

Day 2, preferably, should involve active, occasionally passive recuperation, nervous and physiological. It is a day of low intensity work. Active recuperation involves light exercise and some technical skill practice; passive recuperation will involve massage and baths. **Time**: one to two hours.

On Day 3, players will be involved in a review of tactical considerations exposed during the last match, technical practice and 'on the practice pitch' revision of team play in functional, tactical practice. **Time**: Two to three hours in sessions of 45 minutes per session. Level, moderate intensity.

On Day 4, players will be involved in team practice with the emphasis on group tactical moves within team play: individual technical practice and, say, **ENDURANCE**: speed practice and training. If there are needs for specialized training without any involvement of soccer skills, it will take place on this day. **Time**: Three to four hours in sessions of 45 minutes per session. Level, high intensity.

On Day 5, players will practice match play in four periods of twenty-five minutes each period: group technical practices lasting for one hour in three twenty minute sessions and **SPEED**: endurance practice and training which will last for 45 minutes. The whole day's preparation will take four hours approximately. Level, high intensity.

On Day 6, the group will rehearse and practice set play tactics: practice tactical moves within and between team groups. e.g Mid-field players and strikers, midfield players and backs, between two strikers and one or more mid-field support players and so on will last for one hour in twenty minute sessions. One hour will be spent on weak technical skills and/or weaker foot techniques and one hour will be spent on **SPEED** techniques e.g. **REPETITION RUNS**. **Total**: three hours. Level, moderate to intense.

On Day 7, preparation will occupy two to three hours and will involve set play rehearsals for thirty to forty-five minutes, basic team tactical matters in practice for thirty to forty-five minutes, 'on the pitch' review and analysis of the next day's opponents for half an hour finishing with thirty minutes approximately of individual technical work. Level, low intensity.

A preparation week will involve the players in a total of fifteen to nineteen hours which will include inter sessional rests of ten to fifteen minutes. Many clubs in England feel that the excessively lengthy English season requires players to spend more time resting than practicing and training. This is nonsense and flies in the face of all that is known about human athletic performance. Spread over a working day of eight hours with periodical rest intervals and including a substantial mid day break for food, the weekly program set out will enable player preparation to proceed to optimum effect. If, on the other hand, players are used to having all preparation crushed into a two and a half hour morning, as many in Britain are, the effect will be training and practice 'indigestion' and ultimately chronic player sickness of the whole practice and training business. Preparation for soccer should be pure pleasure, not punishment.

Mid-week matches.

Mid-week matches (two matches in a seven-day-cycle) which occur frequently seriously interfere with planned preparation, nevertheless they are not an excuse for dispensing with purposeful work. The certainty is that if the levels of intensity and quality in practice and training diminish, form and fitness will suffer whatever the number of matches involved.

During a season it is difficult, almost impossible, to recover peak form and fitness levels after major decline has been permitted and the belief that repeated match play will maintain those levels is likely to have been determined more by the coach's social arrangements than by his team's needs. In fact the intrusion of and disruption by mid week matches of necessity requires a stepping up of training and practice levels to cope with what will be increased match demands; form and fitness are not improved by resting. The longer the rests the greater the recovery problem. The diagram gives some idea of the principles which should determine the nature of training and practice in these difficult circumstances.

5.35 A Practice and/or Training Session.

The wave principle still holds good within any single period. Broadly speaking a one hour session will incorporate preparation for optimum practice effect. This may be known, mistakenly in my view, as 'the warm up'. In fact it is a period of ten to twenty minutes in which players are prepared gradually, mentally and physiologically for the main purpose of that particular session. Most human beings have a maximum attention span of about twenty minutes, after which concentration, effective attention to the task in hand, begins to wane. It follows that after twenty minutes say the session should involve a change of activity before the session is brought gradually to a close.

Broadly speaking a one hour practice and/or training session will proceed under the following headings.

Introductory Activity:

An activity which is directly related to the subsequent main purpose (or purposes of the session) and which increases in tempo until the main coaching or practice activity is introduced. Often this opening activity will carry over from a previous

session; it should be activity with which the players are familiar.
10 - 20 minutes.

27 Main Objective.

The main thrust of the coaching, practice or training activity lasting for twenty to thirty minutes, to which players will be expected to give maximum commitment. There may be two periods given to major practice or training objectives. 40 - 30 minutes.

Recovery Activity.

This activity will be less demanding but will still relate to the work done in the Objective session. Gradually practice tempo diminishes allowing players to finish the session in much the same relaxed state as that in which they began the work. 10 minutes.

The organizational effectiveness of any single session is vital. The coach must know;
  (a) Exactly how many players will take part.
  (b) The lowest ball to player ratio needed at any stage during the session.
  (c) The practice areas needed at different stages. This may require special areas to be marked out.
  (d) Two or more sets of colored vests for player identification during practice.
  (e) Additional movable area markers. These are saucer like domes in shape about four inches in diameter and brightly colored. Being movable and light they enable a coach to set up and adjust different sized areas for different progressions in practice.
  (f) Shooting targets or goals. If small practice groups are featured, a number of targets or goals will be needed.
  (g) If practice takes place in a large open space of which the coach's area is only a part, soccer balls will often fly long distances during shooting practices for example. Arrangements must be made for the balls to be retrieved by other players or the practice situations devised will have to include ball retrievers. Practices will need restrictions to ensure maximum player involvement and minimal ball retrieving.
  (h) Such other equipment as needed to aid practice effectiveness.
  (i) The certain availability of assistant coaches if necessary.

5.4 The Principles of Effective Coaching.

5.41 Player Psychological 'Types'.

Before dealing with working principles, it may be useful to consider the different personality types which are likely to be found among players. Coaches themselves are different in 'type' and are likely to relate more easily to those players who share many personality characteristics with them. It is dangerous to categorize people nevertheless we all have dominant and rather less dominant traits. Some players are motivated most by what they achieve as individuals. They are rather less committed to team togetherness than others, nevertheless they make vital contributions to team success. Some may appear to be exceptionally selfish in that they take inordinate pleasure out of beating opponents without assistance. Often they even ignore assistance when they should take advantage of it. These are **SELF ORIENTATED** players and often are found among forward players especially goal scoring forwards.

When faced with a scoring chance it is important for a player to concentrate on an effective shot, not with looking around for passing opportunities.

Self orientation shows itself in different ways. It could be the cause of a player selfishly taking a shot when another player is much better placed but it could also manifest itself when a player in a shooting position passes the ball and the responsibility to someone less well positioned to score.

Other personality 'types' gain most satisfaction from successfully combining with other players. These players often seek closer relationships with certain other players away from the game as well as within it. They form special partnerships within the team so to speak. Occasionally the satisfaction gained from combination can be taken to excess: it may become even more important than scoring goals or winning matches. These players are known as **INTERACTION ORIENTATED** players.

Initially at least they are a coach's pleasure to work with: until their drive for interaction opportunities, with one other player say, becomes detrimental to team achievement.

Finally, there are those players who take the greatest pleasure from team achievements. They are often willing to forego any personal aggrandizement for the pleasure of being a part of successful team play and the emphasis for them has to be on winning. We call these players **TASK ORIENTATED**; they are strongly, even mainly concerned with getting the job done successfully. These players are most noticed individually when they can't play. They cause no trouble on or off the field and may be so withdrawn that sometimes the coach may forget that they are there. These players gain and reinforce their self esteem without recourse to others, even to team coaches. They are very private players but a sensible coach always ensures that they know that he knows how valuable their contributions are. He would be unwise to fail to give his personal if private approval and recognition of their value. They do not seek or welcome public plaudits unlike self orientated players but like all of us they do need their contributions to be properly valued by the coach.

All players have some of all three personality characteristics in their make ups but usually one aspect will predominate. Coaching effectiveness, indeed its acceptability by players, depends on the ability of a coach to recognize each individual player's make-up and to treat him accordingly. The factors in the player: coach: team relationship are enormous and infinitely varied.

This is not to say that ignoring any single factor will seriously disadvantage a coach but infinite variety is best treated by applying sound, coaching principles.

5.42 Command.

From minute one of any session, or sooner, the coach must command the attention of his players. His assumption of a commanding role will be assisted when it is clear

to the players that the coach has made purposeful arrangements on their behalf. In other words he has gone to some trouble to make the event worthwhile.

The notion of command will be further enhanced by the coach's manner of organized intention. He will show that he knows the direction he, the practice and the players will take. This in turn will be assured where the coach uses his voice deliberately, with authority and certainty.

5.43 Control.

Having established a practice and activity pattern a coach will proceed to manipulate his group in much the same way as good drivers drive cars. They know where they are going: where the twists and turns (problems) are likely to be: how to be in the right gear, when to speed up and when to slow down (or when to reverse out of trouble): where and when to signal a change of intention and an acute perception of what everyone else on the road is trying to do. Control comes from good planning, a sense of purpose and smooth changes of emphasis.

A good coach will improve his control, much like a good driver, by practicing his stops and starts. Practice to be effective must be realistic; realistic practice must be controllable, almost instantly, so that both players and coaches can identify where they are, what is and what should be going on in any particular situation.

Too many stops and starts of course put too much strain on the players; they will only accept occasional stops.

At the journey's end the players will feel relaxed, comfortable and better for the experience.

5.44 Persuasion.

A sound coach will proceed by persuasion rather than by compulsion. Initially, he will persuade players of the need for change, if it is needed!

Change may be major, involving the whole team: significant involving a unit of players e.g. strikers, mid-field, back defenders and so on or minor involving one at most two players.

The smaller the unit of players to be the focus of change, the greater the care the coach must take in persuading all the players that change will be worthwhile. This will be achieved when the players, preferably all of them, clearly understand why any change is in all their interests and that it is the responsibility of everyone to encourage and assist in promoting the change. Occasionally, a coach may have to pressurize a player into playing differently or acknowledging a weakness. In the first place he will try 'one to one' persuasion but failing that he may then try to persuade the reluctant player through team friends. In the event of continuing resistance the coach may seek the support of all the players. If this should fail that player may have to be replaced which would be better done with the tacit approval of the rest of the players. A coach should resort to his ultimate authority demonstrably, reluctantly and when there is no alternative.

Dictatorial coaches rule by fear; they may gain short term success. Long term success will be developed through the sensible, intelligent treatment of players: coach satisfaction most certainly will.

A good coach rarely uses intimidation and then only as a final resort with a very difficult player. A tiny proportion of players will be very valuable and very difficult. A coach has to weigh up the pros and cons and act accordingly.

Valuable but difficult players have a habit of getting rid of their coaches before their coaches get rid of them.

5.45 Direction.

A coach must see what players cannot see but from both points of view. It is how the players see their problems and possibilities which leads to change and improvement. A coach should direct their attention, sometimes forcefully. Certainly he must direct their efforts towards successful individual, group and team play; that after all is the essence of coaching.

Perceptive coaching will direct players in the use of every relevant sense, sight, hearing, touch or feel and even smell, to induce improved skill. Coaches are in the business of expanding and extending the full range of players' perceptions of the game. Results are vital but it is a poor coach who fails to direct the awareness of players to the infinite pleasure to be gained from the pure, sensory experience of soccer played well.

5.46 Reward.

Players play for different reasons. Satisfaction can be highly personal and to that extent rarely revealed. A coach must find out what makes each of his players 'tick' and understand the different motivations which cause players to try to play well or indeed to play at all. Whatever caused players to take up the game in the first place may seem to change but basic motivations are never completely lost. Knowing how to reward (acknowledge) a player's achievement in training, practice and play is a powerful instrument for any coach. The use of incentives and rewards to motivate players is a skill of its own: sometimes it is overdone .

Players should be shown how to develop their motivations from the primitive to those involving more sophisticated aspects of self esteem. diagram 3. This is a part of player education and reflects advanced player management skill; through it a coach will learn a lot about his players and even more about himself.

5.47 Consistency.

Coaches who evaluate progress objectively and regularly, and it is a poor coach who doesn't, must be consistent. They sit in permanent judgment of their players; they select them and thereby they are implicitly and explicitly their players' principal critics. We have seen how important it is for coaches to take players into their

The Maturation of Human Needs

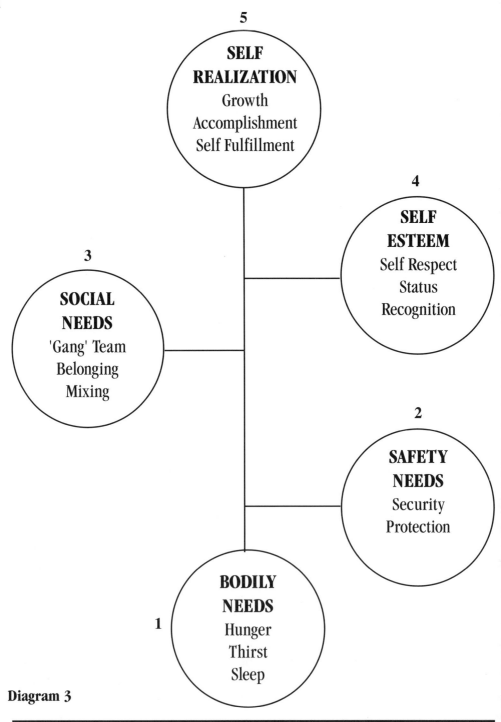

Diagram 3

confidence and to set out for each of them where they stand, where they are going and how they will get there. The coach is the judge and jury; above all else he must be fair in his judgment and absolutely consistent. In matters of personal conduct and behavior, with or without the prior agreement of all members of the team, the coach must be firm, occasionally even severe. First and foremost, he must be consistent in his firmness or severity. Even coaches who rule through fear and intimidation will be acceptable, to some extent, so long as they are consistent.

Unpredictability in a coach is unacceptable and, to the players, unforgivable. Players have enough problems with what they imagine to be the fallibilities of their own skill without having to put up with inconsistencies in their coaches.

Inconsistency seriously destabilizes team, player and coach relationships: there's no future in that.

5.5 Coaching Style.

Having seen many of the world's best soccer teachers and coaches I can say with confidence that they were all different but essentially the same!

- All of them established, very early in a coaching session, their purpose.
- All stated what they required of players briefly and precisely.
- Most took players through rehearsals carefully.
- All transmitted confidence, outright or by insinuation, in the abilities of players to achieve what was required of them.
- All, when faced with player failure, accepted most or all of the blame; none criticized individual players outright other than with those players' prior consent!

Bad coaches are never wrong and always castigate their players for performance errors. Half-time crockery throwers should be in fairgrounds not in soccer.

The best coaches took practice and match pressure off players by joking with them but only up to a clearly understood limit. Beyond that limit play and practice became very serious to all concerned.

All gave players credit and recognition for their efforts, however modest their success. Many used laconic phrases such as 'Rubbish, but well tried': 'Not too terrible': 'We can only get better': 'What will you achieve when I have taught you how to **REALLY** play?' etc.

Limited praise is better than exaggerated, unmerited verbal rewards. Players should receive fulsome praise rarely, even then it is likely to be grossly exaggerated and delivered semi-humorously.

Praise given when undeserved erodes players' confidence in a coach's ability to make accurate, critical judgments. In the words of President Lincoln, one of America's great coaches, 'You can fool some of the people all of the time and all of the people some of the time but you can't fool all of the people all of the time'.

Outstanding coaches only 'throw' their voices over considerable distances, sparingly: they are not screamers. In some quarters there is a mistaken belief that coaching must involve loud and extravagant language; it shouldn't. Those top coaches known to me preferred to communicate briefly, explicitly and at close range with one player or with a specific group of players. Many included all their players in what was said even though it was directly relevant to only one or two.

In my experience all the players always want to hear what a respected coach has to say even when it doesn't directly concern them. Coaches gain respect for their ability to say what needs to be said interestingly. That's what educating players should be all about. Top coaches involve everyone in the work in hand, however player specific it may be. Without involvement, two thirds of the players in practice feel ignored; ignored players become bored players; bored players are almost irretrievable. Better, in that situation, to break it all up and start again.

All the outstanding coaches (and teachers), in my experience, were inspiring, and all were exceptionally good at it. Even so they lifted their voices to 'work' their players infrequently; they shouted rarely and then usually to express pleasure at the achievement of an individual or particular group of players some distance away. By so doing they ensured that the most remote players felt that their work was under scrutiny all the time. As I have said, praise should be used sparingly but when given no one should be in any doubt who has earned it.

Most of these high class coaches were almost invisible and rarely heard until they had something positive to say. Very few adopted the circus ringmaster and certainly not the sergeant major style of direction and communication and all were able to say what was needed briefly and incisively. Whenever they sought feedback from the players, their questions were carefully and precisely framed. Questions were never used to intimidate players. Whenever these coaches had something to say, clearly they had thought out exactly what to say and how to say it to achieve optimum effect. They were worth listening to.

Most top coaches have and need a generous sense of humor. Humor derived from soccer situations is acceptable; directed at individual players much less so. A player who becomes a target for the coach's wit is likely to become the target for the wit of the other players. Any player isolated in this way gradually ceases to be an integral part of a team or he becomes the team clown. Either way he diminishes his value as a player. Joking between coaches and players and between players is fine and in its place important but everyone must know when and at what point it has to stop; the coach must know when and how to stop it. A coach must be able to switch from familiarity to whatever distancing is necessary for firm control to be reasserted. He will be able to put an 'edge' in his manner, sharpen his voice, put on his 'business' face and harden his attitude instantly. There has to be an element of apprehension in the relationship between players and a coach (teacher). As I said earlier, the players must never be sure how far they can go with him.

Those then are some of the fundamentals in player management situations. On these and similar foundations good coaches and teachers will adapt their coaching skills to suit different personalities and the unlimited variation of situations in which they must exercise them.

Chapter 6
Soccer Skill
in Theory and Practice.

Priorities.

All players should be trained and given practice according to individual needs at different stages of development. Development should be monitored short, medium and long term and periodical assessments recorded. Occasionally more general approaches may have to be made to training and practice programs but if the consequences of program adaptation are recorded, strategies for player development need not be diverted. Coaches and teachers prepared to establish priorities in player preparation and to work purposefully towards those ends guarantee that skillful players will come through.

No player is the complete product. There is no age at which, with intelligently conceived practice and training, he cannot improve. The continuing improvement of dedicated, veteran, professional players, well into their thirties, is proof positive that even age need not be an absolute deterrent to progress.

Diagram 4, sets out practice and training priorities appropriate for players with ready access to effective soccer guidance and of course to unrestricted practice opportunities. Players, all players, must commit themselves to intensive and sustained practice with and without the presence of a coach. Players who practice only under the direction of coaches have no chance of becoming high class players. While they are waiting for their coach, thousands of other players world wide are coaching themselves by getting on with practice.

6.1 Soccer Skill Defined.

Soccer skills are deliberate, intended actions by which one or more players, with or without the ball, defeat the intentions of one or more opponents. Skill involves judgment, the correct selection from a number of action options.

Coaches and teachers seeking effective practice situations must accept all the implications of that statement.

Soccer skill is best seen and assessed when players play with and against each other. The parts of soccer, even when perfected, do not necessarily make the whole. The components of soccer skill are as follows:

	TECHNIQUES	TACTICAL SKILLS	TRAINING	GAMES
U7	1. Stopping & Trapping 2. Dribbling 3. Shooting 4. Heading	1. Tricking Opponents 2. Disguising Intentions	1. Agility with and without the ball 2. Speed 3. Suppleness	2 v 2 v 2 Three Goals 'in' 4 v 4 in an area 40m X 30m
U10	1. Control to Dribble & Shoot 2. Control to Pass & Shoot 3. Tackling & Intercepting	1. Using 2 v 1 Situations 2. Pass & Move 3. Making Space 4. 'Losing' Opponents 5. Through Passing	1. Agility Speed 2. Speed & Endurance 3. Suppleness	3 v 3 Plus Goalkeepers 6 v 6 Plus Goalkeepers AREA: 40m X 30m to 60m X 40m
U13	1. Control, Aerial & Ground 2. Control to Pass or Shoot 3. Aerial Passing 4. Dribbling	1. Three Player Moves 2. Control to Pass - First Touch 3. Attack Principles 4. Marking	1. Suppleness & Speed 2. Strength & Stamina 3. Agility	3 v 3 Plus G.K. 8 v 8 Inc. G.K. Conditioning Small Sided Games 11 v 11 Area 80 X 50
U15	1. Control & Aerial Passing 2. Dribbling to Pass/Shoot 3. Heading 4. Tackling	1. Possession & Position 2. Mobility 3. Switching Play 4. Covering & Marking	1. Strength & Power 2. Agility & Speed 3. Stamina & Speed	Conditioned Games (Technique) Small Sided Games 11 v 11
U18	1. Technical 'Touch' 2. 'Deceptive' Techniques 3. Dribbling & Shooting	1. Evading Marker 2. 'Direct & Indirect Play 3. 1 v 1 Play 4. Mobility	1. Power & Stamina' 2. Agility & Speed 3. Suppleness	Zonal Games 4 v 4 up to 8 v 8 Full Game Tactics

6.11 The Techniques Of The Game: Ball Related Priorities.

(a) Receiving the ball ie. stopping it and bringing it under
control, using all parts of the body except the hands or arms.

• Dribbling and running with ball to stop, start, change direction and take the ball past opponents deceptively.

• Shooting to hit the goal, past an opponent, to score with either foot, with the head or with any other legitimate part of the body.

• Passing to other players (and receiving passes)or into space easily accessible to them, long and short, in the air, along the ground, with or without swerve or spin and with appropriate weight.

• Heading the ball to score, to pass or to clear the ball in defense.

• Tackling for the ball to regain possession from and deny progress to opponents. Intercepting passes between opponents.

The techniques may be executed in a variety of ways and applied with athletic ability, at various speeds or with gymnastic ability, involving rapid changes in a player's body shape or in its position.

Technical Interference.

The technical abilities of players may be 'pressured' by opponents. Players can confront each other physically (within the laws) and directly interfere with the execution of techniques.

The goalkeeper uses techniques specific to his function but he must also possess the basic techniques of an out-field player; increasingly he is required to play outside his penalty area.

I have set out the techniques of the game in the order of importance to players as I see the game's priorities: some might differ but my reasoning is as follows.

Technical Logic.

Until a player can bring the ball under control surely and safely, he will not have time to use other techniques. He will tend to kick at it hopefully; hope may not be justified.

Young players develop control so that they can dribble and shoot successfully.

As they mature, players learn that combination (inter-passing) between two or more increases the probability of continuing possession.

Among young players (and not so young players!) the ball is frequently airborne and heading it becomes a necessary extension of foot related techniques.

For those taught badly, or not at all, heading remains a fearful (painful) prospect.

Dispossessing opponents (tackling) also is not a readily attractive skill other than to players who have highly confrontational attitudes from early ages. Intercepting passes is likely to have more appeal than tackling; it will be seen as 'cleverer'.

Different techniques within any technical group make different appeals to players. Even mature professionals imitate the technical idiosyncrasies of admired contemporaries. Quite high levels of soccer techniques may seem to be learnable in isolation from the game. Unfortunately there is little guarantee that techniques mastered in isolation from game conditions will transfer, effectively, into match performance. Players must apply techniques while subject to considerable physical interference, even intimidation.

Soccer is a simple game made up of complex skills and devious people.

6.2 Effective Skill Practice.

Effective practice is the repeated rehearsal of an activity as a consequence of which the quality of performance in that activity is improved and more consistently reproduced at progressively higher levels of demand. ie. in match play.

Effective skill practice must conform to certain precepts which govern success in all perceptual-motor skill learning and teaching situations. Perceptual motor skill is skill involving movement and action based upon judgments about the where, when and how of its application.

6.21 Practice Principles.

Players must agree to the need for improvement and the process by which it is proposed to effect it.

Players need immediately and regularly ongoing knowledge of their practice achievements.

Practice should be of relatively short duration repeated regularly and frequently. This is known as distributed practice.

Occasionally, short periods of practice, twenty to thirty minutes say, should be replaced with a single, relatively long, practice period: sixty or seventy minutes, this is called massed practice.

Transfer of the effects of practice into match play is greater where practice has included all or most of the elements by which skill is judged in the actual situation for which it is intended.

  • In practice, players remember their last effort better than earlier ones.
  • Learning is reinforced by successful experience: it is retarded by failure.
  • It is important to ensure that a final practice effort is a successful one.
  • Practice success is reinforced and recalled better when a player receives appropriate recognition for his or her achievement.

Practice (learning) develops a momentum by which progress continues for some time after practice has ceased.

The most important component in soccer skill and therefore in soccer skill practice, ultimately, is the one over which players seeking to be skillful have the least control: the actions of opponents.

Soccer skill may be shown when players move from one position to another without the ball and often without any intention of receiving it; they try to attract opponents into unsatisfactory positions. These are called 'off the ball' moves. Practice should incorporate such possibilities.

Judging when, where and how to use soccer techniques, learning to make correct selections from any number of action options, isn't possible without the presence of opponents.

Soccer techniques then are the specific **PERSONALIZED** actions by which players manipulate or direct the ball according to an intended pattern. They can be demonstrated outside the context of the game. True technical skill, however, can only be demonstrated in the context of a soccer game of some kind.

6.22 Mental Imagery.

Techniques may be learned, initially, partly in isolation from the full skill situation. Some players are so deeply, imaginatively involved in the game that they can play and practice it to some extent in their minds. They create, play in and learn from imaginary soccer situations especially where they practice alone with a ball and maybe a rebound surface. The personal motivation of such people is phenomenal and rare. Techniques acquired in this fashion still have to be transplanted into situations in which the actions of opponents and co-operating players are integral parts of real skill development. Both affect a player's technical skill; both may make him a success or a failure. The sooner that transplantation occurs the better.

World wide, hundreds of thousands of soccer players have developed extraordinary levels of technique but failed to make any impact in serious competitive soccer. Transferring skills learned and practiced in training into game performance is the only real test of a coach's, a teacher's and of a player's skills.

It must be repeated that the basic skill of soccer is the ability of one or more players to play soccer with and against one or more other players. Without this appreciation, the design and management of effective practice is virtually impossible.

Understanding the difference between solo ball juggling or manipulation and effective soccer skill is crucial; pursuit of the former has little to do with achievement of the latter.

6.23 Perceptual Learning and Practice.

The first stage of soccer learning is **PERCEPTUAL** (sensory); it employs the senses: seeing, feeling, hearing even the sense of smell. No soccer player worth the name will forget the 'charge' he gets from the smell of a soccer ball, of soccer boots, of athletic massage oils and so on. All stimulate imagery and are part of the learning process.

(a) Sight.

A player is shown what a technique or a move to be learned looks like.

Demonstrations should enable players to observe from all relevant points of view; they may be direct, ie. coach demonstrated, player demonstrated or shown on film or video. The important consideration is that attention is directed towards key aspects of performance and the player should be inspired or challenged to imitate them.

It is dangerously easy for a player's attention to be drawn to the style of a performance rather than to key points in execution. Style is acceptable as icing on the cake but too much icing makes the cake not edible.

Players highly capable of visualizing skill internally and able to call up mental images of what to do and how to do it are called visiles.

(b) Touch.

Other players learn quickest from actually 'doing' the skill, however crudely, in the first instances. They need to feel their way through the actual motor experience, often in slow motion. They develop a neuro-muscular feel for a skill. These players are called motiles. Clearly all players learn initially through a mix of sensory experiences.

A coach's know-how will enable him to direct players' attention to key causes of sensation (feel) by which they will be guided during the execution of a skill. That is why it is important, if not vital, that coaches should have had relevant playing experience. Without it they will lack the insight necessary for directing players' perceptual experience.

(c) Hearing.

Players learn when they are guided while engaged in practice. The coach comments constructively on key aspects of performance the correction of which will bring success. It is unlikely that a coach will have this diagnostic ability without having had similar experiences.

It is not impossible to become a soccer coach without playing experience but it is so much easier with it.

Learning by seeing, doing and by hearing are the main perceptual connections in the learning process. Some players find their learning reinforced by the sound made when the ball is kicked or played in a certain way. Players report a consciousness of changes in air pressure and an awareness of movement as unseen opponents move to challenge them. 'Vibes' play a bigger part in most games than many would acknowledge. Most players, however, seem to learn new techniques best by either seeing or doing, or a combination of both. Single or pair rebound practice against a wall or fence, soccer drills and related practices are examples of perceptual learning. Perceptual learning and practice is necessary at all stages of soccer development, bottom to top, but more at the bottom than at the top.

Perceptual, technical practice is a means to an end but not an end in itself. Coaches who fancy themselves as ring masters enjoy putting their players through technical routines, some of them extremely complicated. Their contribution to players' improvement in match play is likely to be more imaginary than real.

Many contemporaries recall hours spent practicing with a tennis ball against a wall — but the same players, when pressed, confessed to spending much more time playing 'pick up' games with and against other players. That is the kind of practice which is the guarantee of progress and of acquiring true skill. Playing 1 v 1, 2 v 1, 2 v 2, 3 v 3 and so on becomes a way of life: to some, all of it! Interestingly, most top players of my generation and earlier seem to have played little eleven a side soccer before adolescence.

6.231 'Staging' Individual Perceptual Practices.

The following are examples of staged, progressive practices. A stage will be used where player progress or lack of it show need. Some players will miss certain stages as they find more relevant levels of learning. Coaching should be adjusted to the actual responses of players, not with putting them through a convenient routine of activity.

Receiving the ball (controlling) and passing.

(a) In an area 30 yards long x 20 three players pass the ball to each other along the ground. Receiving a pass, players try to pass the ball on within a set number of touches but never less than two: one to control, one to pass .

Depending on player response, the coach will emphasize,
- relaxation and withdrawal of controlling surface.
- 'opening' the body's controlling position to enable a player to control and pass with minimal touches.
- as confidence grows, players should look in one direction and pass in another.

Deception should be a fundamental element in all soccer practices at very early stages, if only as an idea.

From ground passing, players move on to deal with low and progressively higher bounces. Teaching points remain the same or similar. The pattern of activity may become more complex.

(b) The players may then develop a game related movement pattern.
A passes to B who, with the minimum of touches but not less than two, passes to C. Having passed the ball each player follows his own pass and runs round the back of the player to whom he passed it. He may receive a return pass, he may not but here we have the beginnings of positional interchange.

Alternatively A, with the ball, runs past B but back heels the ball or stops it with the sole of his foot as he passes to B. B continues the movement with C and so on.

These unopposed 'related' practices are derived from patterns of movement taken from the game.

(c) Progression may be achieved by introducing an opponent D. The three continue practicing controlling, passing and moving but technique may now be subjected to interference. Activity thereby changes from a technical exercise to a skill practice. It involves technique used with judgment of what an opponent may do.

A condition (special rule) may be introduced whereby, having passed, a player must move in advance of the ball to offer himself as a passing option to the player with the ball. He may or may not get it.

Should interference by the opponent cause practice performance to deteriorate, that player might be asked to avoid actually stopping a pass or moving too close to a receiver.

In the early stages of skill practice, opposition may have to be controlled.

Heading.
Here three players practice a throw, head, catch sequence.

A throws the ball to B who heads to C who catches the ball. C then repeats the sequence, C to A to B and so on. This is pure technique practice.

Practice progression might be for the movement to be carried out on the run then in a confined area wherein other threes are moving about practicing the same activity pattern.

Progression: In an area 40 yds. x 20 three players practice against one opponent D, who may intercept only with his head.
The inter-passing players try to achieve a set target of successful sequences.

Progression: The sequence is changed. A throws to B who heads to C who controls the ball using a soccer technique before passing to A or B. Receiving a pass, A or B join C in trying to achieve a set number of passes, five say, at which time the sequence begins again.

Again, this is still substantially perceptual practice. The players have limited requirements of technical skill and learn by seeing, feeling and by doing.

Practice of this kind can be adapted, easily, into more complex practices and eventually into small sided game practices; there begins the need for highly skilled judgments.

Effective skill practice must acknowledge the principles referred to earlier. The greater that acknowledgment the more successful the practice. Where the situation for which improvement is sought is complex, e.g. involves two opposing groups of players (two or more practicing against two or more), the parts into which the action picture is broken down for practice purposes should be as large as possible.

The aim (the intended change in performance) and the objectives (the practice 'routes' by which the aim will be achieved) should enable a coach to set progress 'markers'. These enable players to measure their achievements during and after the completion of practice. 42

Putting together moves and skills is like assembling a jig-saw puzzle or if you like a map. To solve the jigsaw you first look at the full picture inside the box lid. In soccer, that picture is a large piece of the action, a phase of play. Within that phase of play are skills and moves, to be learned and practiced. They are equivalent to the small pieces of the jig-saw. The coach and players build up the practice 'pieces' until a reassembly of the whole phase shows the required change and improvement in performance. The coach continually refers the players to the whole picture in his practice organization so that he and they can see and feel how change in skill improves the whole performance. The most effective method of completing a jig-saw puzzle is by putting together large sections of the puzzle and then assembling these sections to complete the whole picture. The same principle applies in setting up soccer practices. The larger the sections of soccer action which, when put together, produce the desired move or skill successfully, the better.

Learning and applying new skills and moves is rarely a straight forward business. Obstacles to learning will occur and sometimes the group will move back a stage or two in practice before progressing. Some players are very quick learners and able to jump one or two rungs in the ladder of practice difficulty. Perceptive coaches look for obstacles and opportunities and adjust degrees of practice difficulty accordingly.

That's the difference between coaching players and coaching soccer.

6.24 Preceptual Practice.
Precepts are principles and it is important for players to understand the principles behind all soccer action. That is the only basis for understanding the game, a base from which players may eventually coach themselves and develop their own soccer ideas.

Here is an example.
A coach and his players agree that attacking moves developed off the main strikers are not working well. They have identified the problem 'picture' as that in diagram 5, Attack might improve if the players could apply the following principles.
   1. Attackers near the penalty area may be more effective when they drift rather than move quickly to receive passes.
   2. Passing players must support their own passes closely and quickly.
   3. At least one striker inside or near to the penalty area should drift against the flow of attacking play.

   These principles will do for now. The group will discuss development possibilities and how they might improve attacking play in this phase of play.

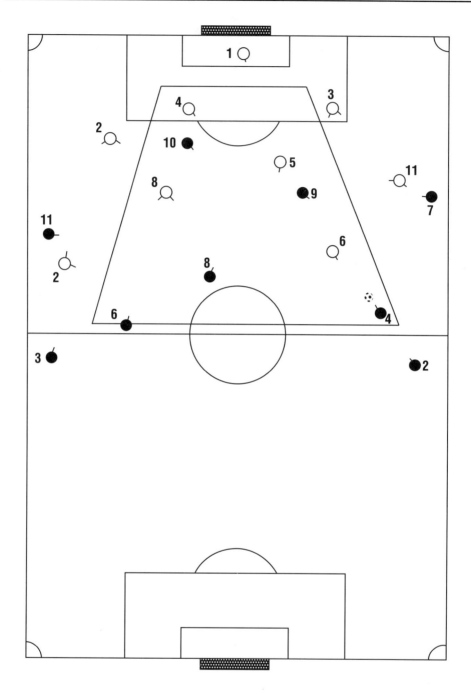

Diagram 5. The use and development of strikers not working well. Identifying 'the picture'.

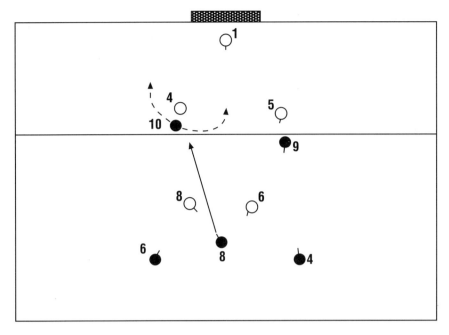

Diagram 6. Focus on the players actually involved in practice development. Shadow practice might be developed by removing all the white players, No. 1 excepted.

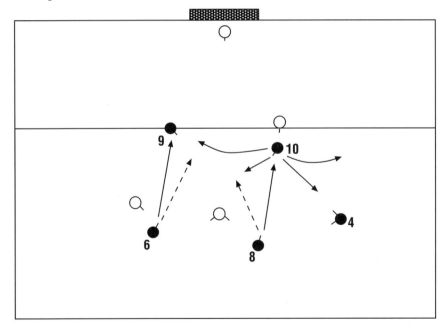

Diagram 7. Reproduction of limited and controlled opposition.

Stage 1. As in the diagram 6, black mid-field players, 4, 8 and 6, look for opportunities to play the ball to either of the strikers, 9 and 10, and thereby to create shooting opportunities.

Players 9 and 10 have a number of options.

    (a) Either player, 9 say, if he isn't tightly marked, may control the ball, turn and run it or pass towards the goal.

    (b) If marked, 9 may 'lay off' a pass, first or second touch, to a supporting player, 4, 8 or 6, from mid-field .

    (c) Alternatively 10 may 'flick' a pass on by head or foot to the other striker behind him.

    (d) A pass to 10 might be 'faked' and delivered beyond him to the further striker, 9. That player might inter-pass with his team mate or develop play through supporting mid-field players.

There are other options but those will do for our purposes here.

Match play (and practice) success will depend on the ability of the leading players to 'do' certain things reasonably well. One or the other of the strikers, 9 say, may lack the required quality of technique to 'lay-off' passes in different directions with variable 'weighting'. It may seem logical to remedy this weakness before practicing any complex piece of interplay. A more productive procedure might be:

    (a) To involve all the players in a 'shadow' rehearsal of a move and of one of the available options.

    • A 'shadow practice' takes players through certain required actions against **IMAGINARY OPPONENTS**. They do so using all the actions they might use in the game and at the appropriate speeds or variations of it.

    • Soccer shadow practice is much the same as a boxer's shadow sparring practice. It is not unlike a live blackboard.

In diagram 6, all the white players except the goalkeeper would be withdrawn to produce a shadow situation.

When the players show that they understand the objectives and that they know how, where and when to use the necessary techniques satisfactorily, controlled opposition may be introduced. Diagram 7.

It is crucial that coaches understand the importance of teaching players not only HOW to execute skills and moves but also **WHERE** and **WHEN** those skills and moves are best used.

Initially, an opponent (or opponents) introduced into practice may offer only token resistance. He may move realistically against play without actually interfering with it. Any player working at a technical deficiency, initially will not be opposed. Trial and success not trial and error is the name of a coach's business. . . and the players'!

The move and an option, or options, will be repeatedly rehearsed over the practice period, twenty to thirty minutes. The players will be free to select which of the action options they will use in each practice 'run'. The existence of one additional action option ensures that opponents cannot predict absolutely what the attackers will do; practice is as realistic as it can be.

The most important consideration of all in judging the effectiveness of practice is the extent to which players are successful. The final run-through during a practice session must be successful. Players remember their final practice best, whether successful or a failure.

Here, as the attacking group shows increasing competence in selecting and using options, more opponents are introduced: one at a time usually. If the introduction of another opponent causes the attacking group to fail once or twice, opposition will be reduced until the attacking group is once again successful.

In the early stages of advanced practice and coaching of this kind, judgment of performance, success and failure, must be down to the coach. He will set the criteria by which practice progress will be measured and he will inform the players what they are. Better still, in a group familiar with modern coaching methods, the coach and the players concerned will discuss and agree the criteria between them. Obviously judgment will be at levels which generously allow for success; there's nothing to be gained from failure. . . other than more of it!

Here is another example of practice construction. Practice stages are represented diagrammatically but all the rungs in the ladder of progression may not be needed and backward steps may need to be taken before players progress.

Good coaches prepare for most (all) eventualities but players indicate where, when and how progress should be attempted.

Problem.
The four back defenders are unsure when and how to mark tight and when to cover. No player has knowledge of a sweeper's role and function.

The coach should seek agreement on the defending principles which affect the issue. These might be to,
- make opponents play 'in front' of them.
- prevent opponents in possession of or receiving the ball turning with it towards goal.
- deflect opponents play into wide positions.
- without someone to mark cover someone who has.

Stage 1. (Diagram 8)
The three white forwards are asked to play as far upfield as they can and to inter-change position across the attacking front frequently. Cross-field moves pose marking problems for backs required to mark attackers and fill space.

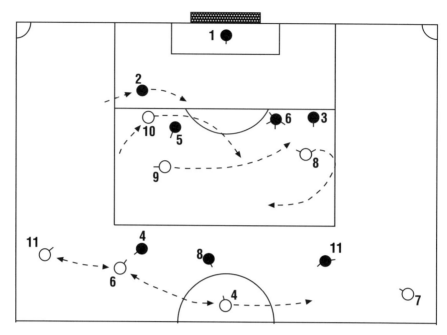

Diagram 8. When to mark. When to cover.

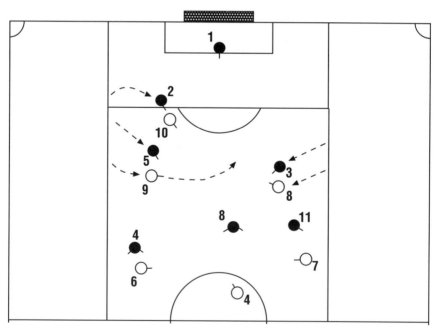

Diagram 9. Strict man-to-man marking among the backs. Black 6 temporarily withdrawn.

Stage 2. Diagram 9

Movement and play is confined to the width of the penalty area initially. One of the central backs is withdrawn from the practice and the others asked to mark tightly on a man to man basis.

This produces a 6 v 6 practice, excluding the goalkeeper.

White mid-fielders are asked to deliver forward passes to the feet of whites 8, 9 and 10.

White 7, 4 and 6 can move forward but not into the penalty area.

The coach waits for a situation which allows him to focus on the need for a central back free enough to control the others and to cover wherever a break through seems possible.

Stage 3. The withdrawn back is reintroduced as a free covering back.

He is required to move with the flow of attacking play, encouraging the markers to direct their opponents away from goal.

The free back's role will be to watch for slack marking, unmarked opponents or opponents with speed superior to that of their marker.

He will be coached in the different action options involved.

It may be necessary to reduce the numbers and limit the space further if focus on a simpler situation is required. e.g. the specifics of tight man to man marking.

With senior players the space to player ratio might be as low as 100 square yards to one player when practice is in or near to the penalty area.

Stage 4. The coach or another player from behind the half way line may occasional-

ly try to deliver long passes behind the backs and to, one side or the other of the sweeper. This 'serving' player may play 'to feet' or into space behind the backs for alert attackers to move onto. This tests players' judgment and speed in 'closing down' on players or 'dropping off' to cover. One attacker may move towards the feeder and the other may turn to run into space behind defenders. At this stage the group will not be concerned with fine judgments of offside moves.

As attackers' are given freedom to act, attackers or defenders may be given confidential briefings by the coach. Coaching at this level is all about setting and solving problems.

Stage 5. An area 70 yards wide and 80 yards long is divided into four zones each

zone 20 yards deep. Diagram 10.

Each team has four defenders, three attackers and a goalkeeper.

The attackers and defenders start in their respective central zones, 4 v 3.

    (a) Initially players cannot cross the half way line. Later one defender may do so.

    (b) No defender is allowed into an END ZONE (shaded) until the ball has been played into that zone or until an opposing attacker has run there.

    (c) Passes from defenders to attackers must be on the ground; later they may also be in the air.

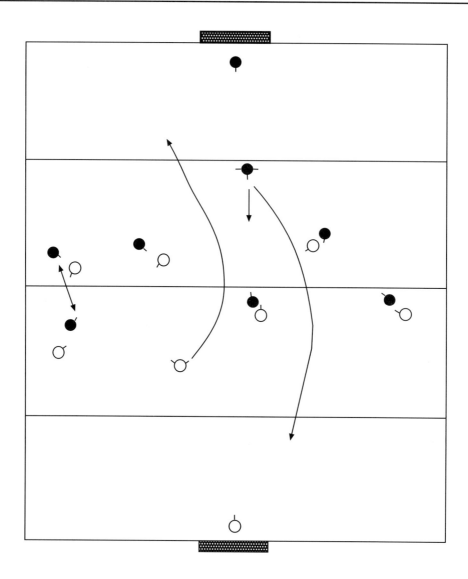

Diagram 10.

This is a conditioned, small-sided game testing the marking and covering skills of two groups of players. There is no reason why, for young players, the same activity shouldn't be used for elementary marking and covering practice 2 v 1 or 3 v 2 say. The width of the area would be reduced to 30 yards for the first and expanded to 50 yards for the second. Here I have used five stages; there could be more or fewer according to the needs and the responses of the players.

The coach will note any technical deficiencies which significantly affect a player's effectiveness. Remedial practice should be instituted accordingly. For example, one of the backs may have an agility problem. Agility speed is a normal training objective but this player may need special attention. Time must be found for suitable coaching, practice or training.

Another of the backs may need to improve his jockeying and tackling skills in 1 v 1 situations. Practice situations will be set up to remedy this and similar deficiencies.

Some coaches advocate always working in match situations with large groups of players. This is possible only for very experienced coaches: those who know when and how specific learning situations can be created and controlled. Even so, small groups in practice enable coaches to see more of the detail in performance; detail which, when missing, makes high quality performance and soccer progress at best difficult, at worst unlikely.

6.25 Preceptual Development

Learning to apply principles (precepts) of play, in practice and in the game, should be built upon a sound perceptual base. Given that players have acquired a good range of technical skills, perceptually, by doing, feeling and seeing those techniques, they should be taught to think about the circumstances in which those skills might be best used. At certain stages of development, understanding the individual and the collective principles of attack and defense are important preconditions to understanding the game as a whole. Without the application of certain principles, team play may be based upon the coach's or, even worse, the players' whims and fancies. If it is the former, the coach can only regurgitate what he was told to do as a player or what he sees other teams doing. In England re-gurgitation is commonplace.

Some coaches become dedicated followers of fashion to cover up their own tactical illiteracy.

Perceptual methods are invaluable when refining known techniques by teaching players to use techniques bilaterally or when introducing new technical options. A few players begin to think deeply about the 'how and 'why' of skill and play at quite early ages. They will understand the application of technical principles relatively easily. Others, experienced professional players included, may have difficulties in accepting new ways of looking at actions which seem, to them, to have come naturally. In such cases it may be useful to relate soccer technical precepts to techniques, in which they are interested, taken from other sports.

Chipping a pass to maximize loft while causing back spin to 'hold' the ball when it lands is a difficult and valuable soccer technique: in principle not much different from chipping the ball in golf. At certain stages in their careers, top soccer players may be more intrigued by the problems of golf than by those of soccer. The transfer of interest and understanding from one to the other may produce the motivation for serious and related practice of both.

6.251 The Principles of Attack and Defense.

The principles as I devised and applied them are as follows:

They provide a sound basis for coach and player education and development and an effective one for match analysis. These terms or terms derived from them have become part of world soccer's lexicon; with the passage of time, one or two may have become distorted in meaning. Preceptual practices involve opposition of some kind, active or passive.

The principles of play involve the exploitation or the destruction of effective spatial relationships between players.

For example, where attacking play seeks to create and exploit the space necessary for success, attackers **DISPERSE** or spread out. Where defensive play, on the other hand, seeks to restrict the space (and the time) available to attackers, defenders **COMPRESS** play or squeeze opponents into tight areas in which they are easier to control. Where a defense is careful to **BALANCE** itself against the likelihood of penetration, especially near to goal, the attack will use **MOBILITY**, interchanges of position, to create imbalance and make **PENETRATION** more likely. Balance is best achieved when individual defenders are in close co-operation with the same team mates in the same parts of the pitch. Defenses can be unbalanced when opponents move into unusual positions in surprising circumstances. Defenders, often, are disconcerted when drawn into unusual positions or unfamiliar, positional relationships.

Familiarity, in soccer, breeds **content**!

Sorry about that, but contentment is the forerunner of tactical inertia.

6.252 Principles of Individual Play.

The higher one goes in the game the more likely it is that certain action options will produce success; other options in the same situations will not.

To take an extreme example, players who inter-pass across the face of their own goal or near to it are likely to be acutely embarrassed when a pass is intercepted. Watching for such indulgence, opponents will make every effort to pressurize players and to intercept the ball. Clearly one side will be punished for risk taking while the other might benefit from it.

A principle of individual play therefore must be that players do not put ball possession at risk near to their own goal. The nearer they are to their opponents' goal, the more justifiable the risk. Players should never be constrained by rules written in stone but certain actions will involve more (or less) risk than others.

Players who have a good idea what each is likely to do in most foreseeable circumstances will be more successful than those made up of 'off the cuff' individualists.

6.253 Individual Attacking Principles.

Players should shoot when they are better than fifty percent
certain of hitting their target with accuracy and force, in that order.

 • Attackers should saturate high probability shooting and scoring areas, diagram 11, whenever the ball is likely to arrive.

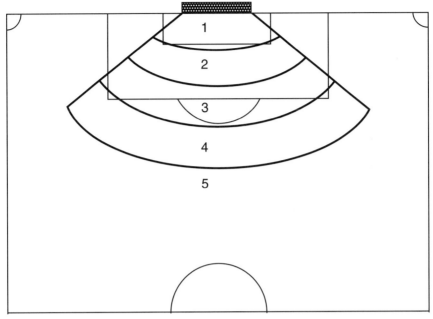

Diagram 11. Profitable shooting zones. The lower the number the higher the scoring probability.

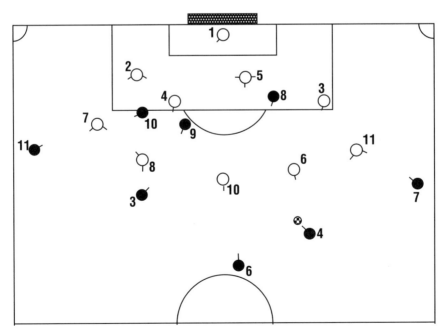

Diagram 12. Black 8 ,9 & 10 are positioned 'inside' white defense. Black 7, 4,6, 3 and 11 are 'outside' white defense.

• Attackers should position themselves to make receiving and turning with the ball as easy as possible.

• Attackers should seek positions and positional changes which test the concentration and comfort of opponents.

• Having given a pass, a player should move to a better position to show himself for a return pass.

• Unlikely pass receivers should draw opponents away from important areas of defensive collaboration and from probable areas of penetration.

• Whenever possible, attackers should position themselves to receive passes inside the opposing defense.

• With the ball and having beaten a defender, a player should attack the weakness created, by passing or running the ball at or through it.

• The nearer they are to their own goal the less players should indulge in 'square' passing.

• The further away from their own goal, the greater the justification for risks taken by attackers, having lost the ball, to regain possession .

Those are some of the precepts within which I would coach attacking play.

6.254 Individual Defensive Principles.

• Defending players must prevent shots at goal

• In mid-field and forward positions, pass receivers should be prevented from turning with the ball.

• Attempts to pass towards shooting areas should be resisted strongly.

• Defenders should intercept or tackle only when success is worth the risk.

• Attackers should be compelled to play outside a defensive structure and prevented from receiving passes inside it.

• Opponents with the ball should be contained for the convenience of defense as a whole.

• Defenders should pass from wide to central positions, ie. from outside in, with minimal risk of interception: preferably none at all!

• An opponent moving through and behind defenders must be marked touch tight until his movement offers no further threat.

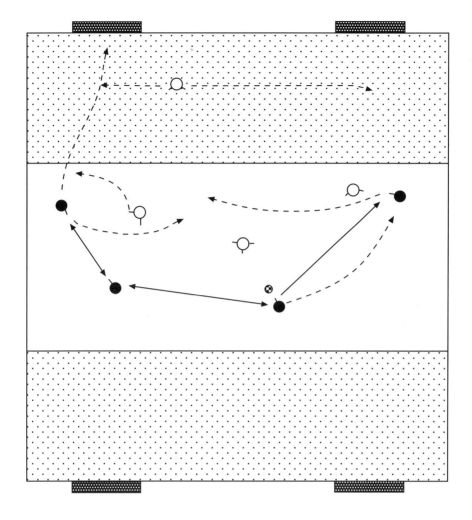

Diagram 13. Conditioning game for stretching play sideways to achieve width.

6.255 Preceptual (functional) Practices.

The situations described are hypothetical but realistic. It is difficult to theorize about practice at this level because players' responses determine what the coach will do next.

The following are assumed to be reasonable practice objectives.

(a) To disperse attacking play and use dispersion to unbalance opposing defensive organization.

Using the whole of the pitch to maximize space available in different phases of attacking play receives lip service from coaches and players who consider it too obvious to warrant practice attention; they are wrong.

In English soccer for more than two decades the whole game was compressed into one sixth of the pitch. Most players required to play skillfully in non-existent space quite simply disappeared. English soccer became pin-ball soccer aimed, often, at the stratosphere. Players capable of receiving, holding and 'working' the ball confidently and purposefully disappeared overnight almost. Recovery has been long, arduous and as yet only barely noticeable.

Dispersion (Width) in Attack.

In diagram 13 eight players are playing 3 v 3 plus goalkeepers on a pitch 30 yds. long x 40 - 50 yds wide.

Conditions: The team in possession of the ball may use its goalkeeper as an extra outfield player. The goalkeeper of the team not in possession must always be on his goal line. This sets up 4 v 3 play.

If the group has an odd number of players, let's say nine, one player becomes the 'floater', always on the side of the team in possession of the ball. Goalkeepers stay in goal. This sets up 5 v 4 play .

Each team will have the floater as an extra player as possession of the ball changes.

• The advantaged team uses optimum space to draw opponents away from tight, integrated defensive positions. It may use interchanges of position from very wide positions into other very wide positions to disturb defensive positional relationships.

• To emphasize width in attack (an element of dispersion) the following condition might be imposed.

• The rearmost player in possession must always give passes to sideline receivers. Failure to do so results in possession being transferred to the other team.

• A player moving 'in field' from a sideline position must continue his run to another sideline position.

• Defending players try to contain attacking play while retaining balance against a breakthrough. Attackers need to know how and when to move close to a balancing (covering) defender in order to affect their decisions.

In diagram 13, a goal is scored when a player runs the ball through either of the two 'gates' at the ends of the pitch.

Condition: The last defender or goalminder cannot defend outside his end zone.

There is no reason why other skill objectives should not be pursued as long as the coach and players are clear that additional objectives are secondary in importance.

Secondary objectives might be:

    (a) Passing: The advantaged team is allowed only three, two or one touches to pass the ball.

    (b) The advantaged team scores extra points for passes made successfully 'inside' opponents. (2 points).

    (c) Any forward player receiving the ball tries to run the ball at and past an opponent (2 points).

    (d) A goal scored by running the ball through either of the two gates scores 3 points; a goal scored by passing the ball through a gate scores 1 point. Points awarded are increased or reduced according to the practice emphasis the coach wishes to promote.

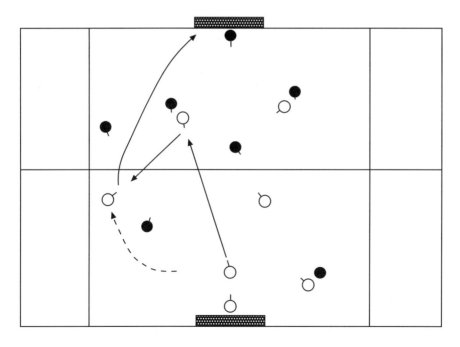

Diagram 14. Defensive containment & penetration in attack.

Mobility (positional interchange) in Attack.

The primary objective is to educate players where, when and how to interchange positions.

Poorly chosen or thoughtless interchanges can disrupt a whole team's tactical balance. Movement for the sake of moving can be the source of serious loss of 'shape', even chaos. When necessary, players must be taught when, where and how to move and how positional interchanges work.

On a pitch 70 yards long x 20 yards, two teams have three outfield players and a goal defender.

Only attackers and the goal defenders may enter the end zones.

The goal defenders may not leave the end zones.

Teams try to penetrate the opposing triangle to run the ball through either of the two end gates.

The 'nose' (foremost) defender and his two supporters try to maintain a tight triangular relationship to keep their opponents from passing and receiving inside the defensive triangle.

Conditions: Attackers pass and follow their passes towards and behind the pass receiver. These are 'loop' runs. The pass receiver must hold the ball, even under challenge, until the loop run has been made. Diagram 14. Then the possession player may pass to the loop runner or take alternative action.

Defenders following the loop runner may leave space for 'inside' attacking options.

Containment in Defense and Penetration in Attack.

On a pitch 60 yds. wide x 40 yds. (Diagram 14) there are six outfield players plus a goalkeeper on each side. Two from each side must be in their forward half of the pitch. The front two may change but there must never be more than two: later only one.

The possession team's goalkeeper may risk becoming an outfield player. A goal scored from a team's defending half scores 2 points and from a team's attacking half 5 points.

The defending players contain their opponents by pushing up close to the mid-line, trying to limit opponents to long range shots.

Condition: When a player moves into one of the wide zones, an opponent must move there with him. Failure to comply with any of the conditions concedes a penalty kick.

Clearly different attacking skills are required: receiving and shielding the ball: turning off a marker to shoot or pass: laying off passes to support players on the edge of the area for long shots.

Defending players must close down opponents quickly to prevent shots and forward defenders try to contain opponents by drawing them away from key areas.

'Conditioned' games are very important in the development of all soccer skills.

They provide controlled realism.

Here are some examples of preceptual practices targeting individual principles of play.

Turning off opponents or inter-passing to shoot.

(a) The practice area is 60 yds. long and 40 yds. wide divided into three zones each 20 yds. deep. This is the approximate equivalent to three penalty areas. There are three players against two in each end zone with two against two in the mid zone. A third ('floating')player in the mid zone is always with the attacking side. When in possession, the goalkeeper may become an outfield player.

Practice Objectives.

Attack: (a) Receiving the ball, or inter-passing to create opportunities for turning to shoot quickly and accurately in or close to the front zone, hence the near equivalence to a penalty area.

Condition: 1. The ball must be played through the mid zone.

Three attackers against two defenders and the goalkeeper in the front zone. Attackers make space in which they can shoot first or second touch.

Condition: 2. Attackers must shoot within four, three or fewer touches. Failure to do so results in the transfer of possession.

With relatively unskillful players, goalkeepers may be omitted or, say, not allowed to use their hands.

Condition: 3. After the ball has been played into the front zone, one mid-field defender may move back into end defense, producing a 3 v 3 situation. Now forward players have less time for turning and shooting.

The coach establishes the relevant principles and player attention is focused on their application in different situations.

Practice can be adjusted by
1. altering the numerical bias,
2. imposing different conditions and
3. offering different scoring incentives.

Using these devices is the key to producing effective practices, especially for advanced players.

Preceptual practice can be used at any level of player development. Effectiveness is governed by the capacity of players to understand and apply principles together with the capacity of coaches for injecting sensible information at the right time.

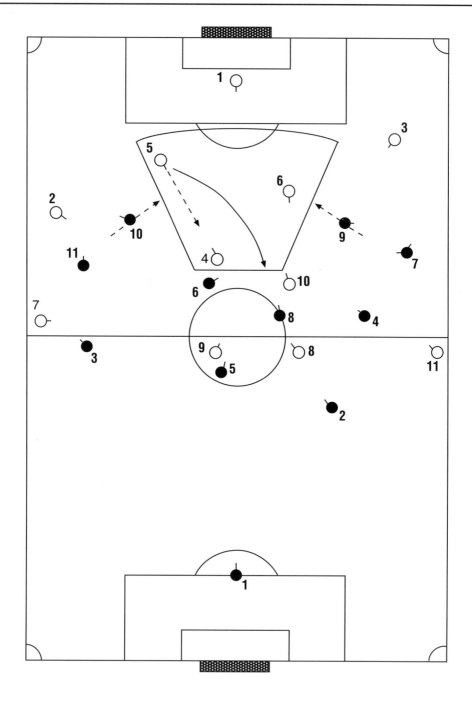

Diagram 15. Early funnelling containment to encourage central attacking development and possible interceptions.

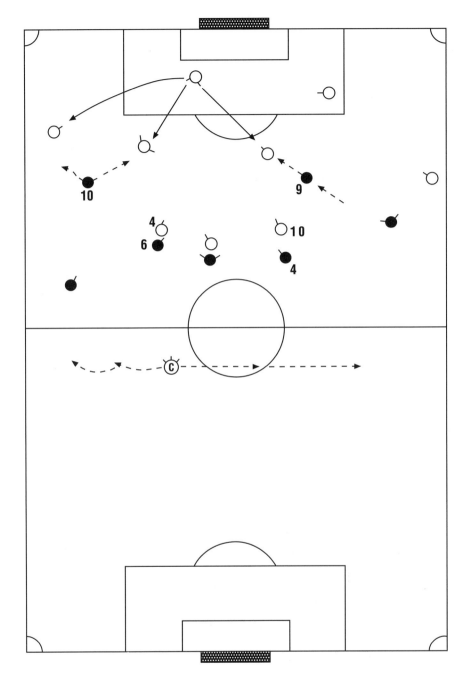

Diagram 16. A phase practice in funneling and containing leading to interceptions.

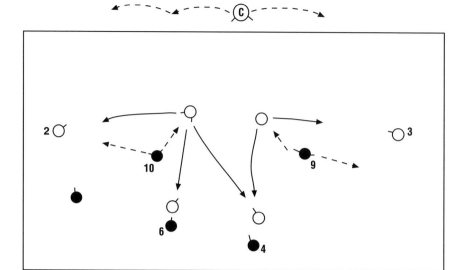

Diagram 17. Progression from Diagram 16. Inviting passes to assist interceptions.

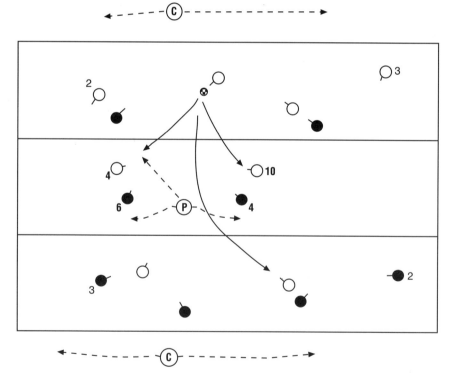

Diagram 18. High intensity intercepting practice.

6.26 Conceptual Development.

Conceptual skill involves the imagination and soccer intelligence needed to solve or set individual and group tactical problems; those problems inevitably involve opponents. Conceptual coaching is based upon situations derived from match play or from a phase of the game. A phase of the game is a large, particular, part of it. A considerable number of players will be involved, sometimes two full teams.
The following are examples.

(a) Counter attack developed from possession regained in the defensive half of the pitch.

(b) Defensive pressure applied to regain possession lost in the opponents' defensive third of the pitch.

(c) Mid-field defensive organization, integrated with back play, to contain opposing attacking play.

(d) The development of attacking play to achieve effective crossing positions and penalty area finishing.

(e) Set play situations (corner kicks, free kicks, throw ins) from either a defensive or an attacking view point.

6.261 Conceptual Practices.

First, a coach needs to identify the problems to be solved; the following might be such problems.

A team has two central mid-field players reliable in winning the ball in defensive situations: no one else is. The team tends to be overrun in mid-field when defending. Ball possession is difficult to regain and therefore counter attacking possibilities are poor.

The coach should want the team, when defending, to play to its strengths thereby enabling the two ball winners to function to optimum effect. Forwards and the wide mid-field players might contribute by deflecting opposing attacking build-up towards the two mid-field ball winners.

In **Diagram 15**, the white team is being encouraged to bring the ball out of defense centrally, The advanced black forwards threaten any attempts for the white backs to play wide. The two black mid-field tacklers mark their opponents less than touch tightly to invite passes to their feet. This opens up a possibility for intercepting or tackling. Other players in mid-field need to be taught to jockey (guide) opponents with the ball 'inside' ie. towards the team's mid-field strength.

If the situation remains unsatisfactory, I might position my best reader of 'game flow' behind the two tacklers as picket (patrolling) player. Covered by a picket player, the two mid-field players would be encouraged to fractionally increase risk when intercepting or tackling.

In **Diagram 16**, the phase practice involves eight against seven.

Stage 1. Beginning with a throw out from white goalkeeper, the eight white players play to pass the ball along the ground into the hands of 'C'. I would establish certain confidential objectives for the black players.

e.g. To ensure that passes from all white players go to the two central white players 4 and 10. Problems would be identified immediately.

The players would be ready for a breakdown of the phase play into relevant practices.

Stage 2. In an area 60 yards wide and 30 yards long.

Players would work on the 'splitting' skills of the two advanced black forwards, coaching them to invite the white backs to play through central mid-field by threatening to isolate any attempt to build up through the wide backs, white 2 and 3.

Mid-fielders, black 4 and 6 would be coached in closing down on their opponents quickly and safely to prevent them turning with the ball. Then they would be coached into inviting passes which might be intercepted. **Diagram 17**.

The white team continues trying to work the ball along the ground into C's hands.

Stage 3. In the same area **Diagram 18**, there are now two equal groups; 4 defenders v 2 attackers in each end zone and 3 defenders v 2 attackers in the mid zone.

White 4 and 10 are always attacking mid-field players; black 4 and 6 together with picket player (mid-field sweeper) P are always defensive. As play switches from end to end, the whole mid-field group merely turns round and plays the other way.

Stage 4. Here I might allow white 2 and 3 to move forward into mid-field should opportunities arise. As they move forward, black 2 and 3 would move forward to confront them. In these circumstances the number of players in mid-field might be 4 v 4 or 3 v 3. The white players would be encouraged to interchange position to try to disrupt the effectiveness of the two central 'destroyers'. The picket player's reading of play would be vital. In the event of black 4 and 6 being drawn apart or into false positions, the picket player must know how and when to seal off central mid-field space and when to pick up opposing attackers who escape their markers.

Conceptually, this is the stage at which the players involved should be coached to play in different positions.

Unless this is done, coaches are tempted to become puppet masters. They rage up and down the side lines pulling the players' strings and making decisions for them. Of course when mistakes occur it's the players who made the bad decisions, never the string pullers!

Decision making, perhaps is the single most important, advanced skill in any team passing game, must be part of a coach's program of player development.

A great coach is one who educates players to levels of 'know how' whereby they can coach themselves.

Chapter 7
Training for Soccer

T raining means different things to different people. I see training as the systematic establishment and sustainment of desirable levels of neuro-physi-ological, anatomical and psychological performance applicable to the game of soccer.

There are five 'S' factors which contribute to 'top' soccer performance, **STAMINA**, **SPEED, STRENGTH AND SUPPLENESS** are four of them. The fifth is **SKILL**; it is by far the most important.

Significant improvement in skill is likely to reduce the need for all or any one of the other four factors.

This is not to diminish the need for fitness in player preparation but training, overdone, is decreasingly relevant to match performance. It may be a serious waste of players' and coaches' time: a great deal of it is. Logic gives skill practice the highest priority in player preparation. Logic, however, is not a noticeable trait of some professional managers.

7.21 STAMINA (endurance).

STAMINA (endurance) enables a player to repeat certain muscular or total body actions as often as required, within the context of the game, without noticeable deterioration in skill quality.

For our purposes there are two forms of stamina.

(a) **GENERAL STAMINA** or cardio-respiratory (cr) endurance.

Where a player collapses from total fatigue, temporarily incapable of any further effort, his **GENERAL STAMINA** (cr endurance) has failed. The failure of general stamina, in a soccer player, is only likely when he is seriously untrained: when he plays in severe climactic conditions, extreme heat or cold or at high altitude or when he is ill.

Oxygen, the fuel of athletic performance, is drawn by the act of breathing air into the lungs, absorbed by the blood, and taken into the heart hence the term cardio-respiratory (or heart: lung) system. Failure follows an inability to take in enough oxygen to enable the heart, itself a muscle and the system's pump, to function effectively.

(b) **LOCAL STAMINA** or cardio-vascular (cv) endurance.

Where a player cannot continue to play because of the refusal of a certain muscle group to function, the calf muscles or the ham string group for example, LOCAL STAMINA (cv endurance) has failed. Failure comes from excessive contraction of the muscle and thereby its failure to relax when required to do so. Localized spasm restricts blood flow to the muscle and without an adequate blood (oxygen) supply the muscle cannot work. Obviously a muscle in a sustained state of contraction (spasm) cannot accept blood and distribute it. The result, usually, is severe 'cramp'.

Generally speaking, adverse ground conditions especially heavy, muddy grounds or unusually thick and 'holding' turf together with unusual running demands bring on cv failure. Highly motivated players, unused to a new level of play and trying to contribute more than they might normally do, are likely victims of cv failure.

In both forms of stamina failure, rest will facilitate recovery. Failure of the cr system can be dangerous and certainly indicates a serious fitness deficiency. Failure of the cv system is easily overcome by rest and massage by which blood flow to and from the muscles in spasm is facilitated. Resumed action, however, is likely to bring about repeated failure in that specific muscle group. The two systems are only treated as separate considerations in this book to suit our needs as coaches and trainers; in fact they are closely integrated.

The cardio-respiratory-vascular system is very important in all sports but especially in those which make persistent, variable and, occasionally, extraordinary demands upon it. Soccer is such a sport.

Sustained, 'total action' practice and training activities play an important part in player preparation especially in the early development of young players. The neurophysiology of the system is a good deal more complicated than the explanation given here but this should suffice. Improving or maintaining the two different forms of stamina requires different forms of training.

7.22 SPEED.

Speed is evident in three different forms in soccer,
- SPEED OF ACTION.
- SPEED OF REACTION.
- SPEED OF ANTICIPATION.

7.221 ACTION SPEED.

• is the speed needed when a player moves his body, with or without the ball, from one place to another by running, jumping or diving. Speed is controlled by the player's ability to decide what action is necessary, to start the movement and to accelerate, as required, in the shortest time. Action speed is adjustable, players may have to receive a pass, give a pass, dribble, shoot or execute any of the skills of the game even against physical resistance from opponents. Obviously a soccer player's action speed is not that of an Olympic sprinter: which begs the question why some coaches train players as if they are.

7.222 REACTION SPEED.

• is needed when a player has almost no time in which to choose what action to take;

he must act (react) instantaneously and he has the minimum of time for acceleration. A goalkeeper needs **REACTION SPEED** when faced with an opponent about to shoot from close in. He has to wait until the last milli-second, for any 'give away' sign from his opponent, before reacting, lightning fast, to block the shot. Similarly a striker receiving a ball deflected off an opponent has no time to assume a well shaped shooting position; he must react to shoot in the limited time available.

7.223 ANTICIPATION SPEED.

• is the insight needed to assess action options available to other players, predict their choices and have the speed to act accordingly. Anticipation gives a start advantage which more than counters the speed of a 'pure' sprinter over a short distance.

Speed of anticipation can be improved only in soccer skill practices, certainly not on athletic tracks. The sharper the player's anticipation, the easier the game becomes. Not a lot of coaches understand the implications of that statement: they should.

Just what is possible for any player in any given situation is gained from acute perception, from experience, from a very long memory and from instant recall. The skill can only be learned and improved through specific practices and perceptive coaching.

Perceptive coaches coach soccer players, not merely soccer; they may be a dying breed.

7.23 STRENGTH (power).

• is required in difficult playing conditions, on heavy grounds, against strong wind, in snow or rain and especially against physically bigger and heavier opponents. These conditions are resistant to a player's movements and skills, hence the demands made on his muscular strength. Size of course isn't necessarily an indication of strength. How, where and when strength is applied are more important than sheer muscle bulk. Certainly the strength needed in soccer isn't the absolute strength of the weight lifter.

Soccer strength is the specific strength required to employ the skills of the game more efficiently and effectively, most noticeably in adverse conditions.

When charging an opponent, shoulder to shoulder, a relatively small player can knock a much larger opponent out of the play if he can apply his strength at the right time, especially when the opponent is off-balance.

POWER.

• is muscular strength applied to overcome resistance at speed.

Resistance, as we have seen, may be produced by opponents, the ball, ground conditions, the wind, the slope of the playing surface, the length of the grass and not least the player's own weight. Power, clearly, is derived from muscular strength. The higher the levels of play the more relevant and useful power becomes. Soccer training designed to improve strength (power) must be closely integrated with speed and stamina training and, as always, with skill. A player may have strong legs but unless he can apply strength powerfully and accurately, when shooting for example, his strength may offer no advantage. Power is shown when soccer players start and accelerate to top speed over very short distances particularly from stationary positions. And here's an important tip for slow starters: cheat!

Get your start in first by keeping on the move, especially when action is imminent.

Power is also needed to explode into a high jump to head for goal: to shoot at long range and, for a goalkeeper, to jump or dive to save shots. Hitting long, accurate passes, in the air but especially along the ground, requires superior kicking power. Apparent effortlessness and therefore deception while executing any soccer passing technique over distance almost certainly calls for controlled power.

7.24 SUPPLENESS (flexibility).

• is the capacity for producing an extreme range of movement within a particular joint (or joints), while executing a skill, without strain or injury. Soccer players occasionally need to stretch or twist their bodies and limb joints into unusual positions to play the ball. They assume unusual body positions because something happens which they have not anticipated. A defender, inside the penalty area and deceived by a deflection, may need to turn and jump into an overhead kicking position in a split second with no thought of personal injury; he reacts and does it, if his suppleness allows. If it doesn't his pain will be instant and obvious.

A goalkeeper, diving left say, may have to change direction for a deflection of the ball to the right. Suppleness allows his limbs to distort in response to unexpected signals. An attacker may reach the ball, skidding across the goal, if he can stretch like a high hurdler and split himself in two, almost, to stretch and score.

A 'stiff' soccer player has severe limitations and the older he is the less his chance of becoming supple. Suppleness comes from exceptional 'bendability', 'stretchability' and 'twistability'; all players need it, just in case! It is achieved by taking a joint to the furthest points in its ranges of movement and then, by patient progression, a little further.

Without suppleness, unusual limb relationships, brought about suddenly and powerfully, may cause the muscles, tendons or ligaments which affect joint movement to tear or snap under the strain. The consequences are very serious; rehabilitation and recovery are long, hard processes; they can be avoided.

The **FIVE 'S' FACTORS**, Speed, Strength, Stamina, Suppleness and Skill all contribute to soccer fitness but Skill is the factor which will pay the biggest dividends given the right sort of attention. And being the most difficult to improve, logic demands that:
  • The greatest proportion of preparation time must be given to skill.

That fact hasn't yet taken root everywhere in the game; it must! A minimum 75 % of preparation time must be devoted to skill: individual technical skills: group skills, both technical and tactical: integrated skills used by large numbers of players in certain phases of play: for example say in midfield defense leading to counter attack: in forward pressing defensive tactics: in 'last third' deep defensive methods and so on and not least at set plays.

If training in any or all of the first four factors, speed, stamina, strength and suppleness does not improve performance in the game, it will have been a waste of time. It may be infinitely easier to train a player than to coach him but the game's future is in coaching.

7.3 Designing Training Activities.

Training must include game elements to ensure that its effects are transferred into better player performance. It may seem, and is, easier to treat physical conditioning as a separate consideration and isolate it from all soccer elements. That kind of training may produce superior athletes but it won't produce better soccer players.

The closer the relationship between training, practice and game skills, the greater the transfer of the effects of training into match performance. The less the similarity the lower the degree of transfer.

Players never show the improvement in game skill to justify the time spent on 'unrelated' training activities. Long periods of running training represent coach incompetence, they certainly don't meet player needs. Trying to train players' minds and bodies separately is seriously unprofitable.

7.31 Principles of Design.

To produce effective training activities a coach must apply certain principles.

Training activities must:
    a.   challenge the imaginations of players.
    b.   inspire a desire to improve.
    c.   conform to known physiological principles.
    d.   progress according to players' responses.
    e.   relate closely to the needs of each player.
    f.   involve activity patterns which have significant similarity to movement patterns in the game.
    g.   enable players to 'feel' or see 'in-the-game' improvement.
    h.   induce confidence in the effects of training.

Skill practices, skillfully adapted, can be used to improve stamina, strength or speed but not all at the same time! 'Conditioned' games are games governed by special rules which are designed to affect the action options of players. Conditioned games can be easily adapted to improve stamina, strength or speed.

Training to increase **SUPPLENESS**, safely, must be strictly controlled; this quality is best developed outside the context of the game.

There are no 'all in one' training activities which develop all the physiological qualities required by soccer at the same time. Coaches who claim to have invented training activities purporting to do so are kidding you, and themselves.

All training (and practice) must observe the constraints of known physiological principles.

For example, speed is significantly improved by practicing running at top speed over relatively short distances a limited number of times; let's say 5 to 8. A player must recover almost fully between each run. This is known as repetition (rep) running.

SPEED: strength is enhanced when a player practices running at maximum speed against a resistance.

Finally, starting and accelerating to top speed is a product of power, especially leg power. These principles must be acknowledged when designing soccer speed training activities.

Speed is developed through quality work not through quantity. The power required to start and accelerate to top speed in the shortest time is best developed when the sprinting action is subjected to resistance. e.g.:
  • sprinting uphill
  • sprinting when carrying extra weight
  • sprinting when pulling extra weight
  • sprinting when pushing against a resistance.
  • sprinting on soft sand or on any 'holding' surface e.g. mud or long thick grass.
All activities should include soccer skills and game activities.

Speed training must involve a ball. It's purpose is to motivate players to work harder and to develop speed actions related to the game. Players need soccer sprinting styles, not those of track sprinters. When playing the ball reduces a player's speed noticeably, the training objective of speed improvement is likely to be lost. Interference must be eliminated if that objective is to be achieved.

It is a waste of opportunity to seek speed, strength or stamina in their 'pure' forms as in track athletics. Soccer's need for these qualities is unpredictable. Nevertheless players should train (and practice) in anticipation of the most difficult demands which they may meet in a game.

In soccer (as in most games), each of the 'S' factors is needed in conjunction with one or more of the others. Stamina is mixed with speed, speed with strength and power. Strength is an important component of stamina, especially local stamina, and so on. Suppleness affects the ranges of different limb movements and thereby the range and quality of many soccer skills.

7.31 Quantifying Training. (How much is enough?)
It is impossible to predict precisely how much work each individual player in a team

will be required to do in any game. Work requirements differ from game-to-game; work capabilities differ from player to player.

A number of 'easy' matches may be followed by an exceptionally demanding one. Also the circumstances governing demand are unpredictable. Injuries to key players may require changes in tactical emphasis. Certain players may need to work harder than normally. Nevertheless we need some criteria by which we can estimate, broadly, the amount of training required. Increasingly, soccer demands 'all round' players, players who play competently and skillfully in most positions. Modern players, looking towards the future, should be prepared for that eventuality .

7.32 Distances (Yardage).

A reasonably hard working player covers something in the order of 6,500 yards of ground during a match. About 4,000 yards at less than top speed, from jogging to striding say, 2,500 yards at considerable speed but only a relatively small proportion of those 2,500 yards at top sprinting speed. If he runs more maybe he is running too much!

The 6,500 yards is spread over the two halves of a match ie. 3,250 yards in each 45 minute period to produce 2,000 yards at moderate pace and 1,250 yards at speed.

A player rarely runs continuously for more than 150 yards and sprints rarely exceed 50 yards and may be as short as 10 yards.

7.33 Moderate Intensity Training. (MIT)

This intensity level varies between jogging and fast striding. Using the distance esti-mates in 7.32, the number of moderate intensity runs (repetitions) required in one half may be calculated by dividing the amount of moderate pace running , ie. 2,000 yards, by the maximum length of a single run, ie. 150 yards. This gives a maximum number of 13 repetitions of 150 yards approximately or, if you wish, 20 reps. of 100 yards. Two work sessions with, say, a five minute rest between each will be the maximum MIT needed.

7.34 High Intensity Training. (HIT)

The maximum number of sprints needed can be estimated by dividing the total dis-tance sprinted, 1,250 yards, by the approximate distance covered in a single sprint, at most let's say 50 yards. This produces the need for a maximum of 25 repetitions of 50 yard sprints or 20 at 60 yards if you wish. A player is unlikely to sprint, flat out, twenty five times over 50 yards in any half.

Sprint 'reps' will be based on the timed sprinting capabilities of individual players. Speed training involves a maximum of six to eight reps. with full recovery between each repetition. It follows that out of a total training target of 25 reps. a large proportion of sprints should be incorporated in the MIT program.

This is relevant since players are often required to sprint as fast as possible when suffering from degrees of tiredness, especially towards the end of a match.

Repetition 'targets' are set and adjusted to meet agreed objectives within the condition of individual players.

Training sessions should be 45 - 50 minutes in duration: 10 minutes warm up and 35 - 40 minutes specific training activity. 3,250 yards of various running activities, involving MIT and HIT levels and including recovery intervals, will take about 25 to 30 minutes; remaining time will be used for 'break' activities, skill practices or small games. Training demand will be significantly greater than in the game and all will involve technique and skill applied under stress. Sustaining high level skill in small-sided game practices during intensive training requires considerable self-control, the control needed in demanding matches. The transfer of the effects of training into match performance will be appreciably improved.

7.4 Types of Activity.

A soccer player runs while preparing to receive the ball, challenge for it, pass it, dribble with it or to use other game skills. Some running involves accepting or avoiding physical challenge. Planning training regimes for soccer players is not as simple as for track athletes. The amount of work done by any player is affected by his ability to 'read' play, to anticipate what is likely to happen, together with the efficiency with which he exercises his skills.

Skillful players rarely work as hard as those less skillful: they don't need to.

The implication for players who dislike training and for coaches who have to deal with them is worth thinking about.

To justify reductions in training levels players, individually and collectively, must become more skillful.

High investment in skill practice and in skill related training will pay off and life may become easier for everyone, except managers and coaches. To increase training efficiency, to produce optimum improvements in the shortest possible time, certain principles must be applied.

7.41 Stamina - Speed Training.

Here the primary objective is STAMINA development, the ability to sustain a large number of 'runs' with the ball, receiving it or passing it, mostly at moderate speed. Speed, here the secondary objective, indicates that into the bulk of MIT there will be injections of HIT.

The intensity of stamina training can be raised by:
- keeping the yardage constant while reducing the time taken to cover it.
- keeping the time constant while increasing the yardage covered.
- increasing the yardage and reducing the time taken to cover it.

7.411 Interval Training.

Interval training involves an interval of relatively intense work followed by an interval of less intense work which enables the player to partially recover (recovery intervals). Work and recovery intervals are repeated an increasing number of times.

Interval training is highly relevant to the needs of a soccer player. The game itself involves similar work and recovery.

During early HIT intervals players aim to raise their pulse rates to about 180 beats per minute, according to the physiological state of each player. During recovery intervals that rate is allowed to drop to about 130 beats per minute. During both phases players should be involved in soccer related action of some kind.

The lower a player's state of training, the higher the ratio of recovery to work. As his condition improves, this ratio of recovery to work is lowered. Most players should eventually work on a ratio of one recovery to one intensive interval. Lowering the ratio of recovery to work beyond 1:1 is likely to be unprofitable.

We don't need Grand Prix cars to take our wives shopping even though modern professional players could afford them.

Players, with exceptional, perhaps even inborn, stamina capacities, need training to be adjusted accordingly. There is no point in putting all players through the same program when they could be engaged in other more beneficial activities. A whole squad training together may seem to improve togetherness but it will do precious little for individual needs. Lazy players will advocate it, resist them, firmly.

Interval (stamina) training aims to increase or sustain the player's oxygen take-up and utilization system. His lung capacity and power for taking in oxygen will be increased as will the volume of blood (oxygen) put into circulation by each stroke of the player's heart. Stamina training should improve the efficiency of the heart: muscle, oxygen distribution and utilization system. It also facilitates the removal of the waste products of physical activity. All these capacities are measurable by any sports physiologist.

Soccer is an AEROBIC (oxygen available) endurance event. Players are never required to play while unable to replenish the oxygen used during performance. Training of ANAEROBIC intensity (oxygen not available) need not be a part of soccer training; players should be delighted to hear this!

Training Activities.

(a) In diagram 19 the 'course' is twice the distance between the two penalty areas on a normal size pitch, ie. 2 x 75 yds. or about 150 yards. The number of repetitions aimed for will depend on players' fitness levels and will be between 8 and a maximum of 13.

13 repetitions of 150 meters will cater for the moderate speed target of 2,000 yards. These moderate speed reps. will be interspersed with a suitable number, say ten, of 50 yards fast sprinting reps.

Soccer teams will find it beneficial to organize squad or team training in small equal groups which will be the basis for training and practice competitions. During interval training, the larger the group, the lower the intensity level of training: the smaller the group the higher the intensity (work : recovery) level. e.g. In a group of

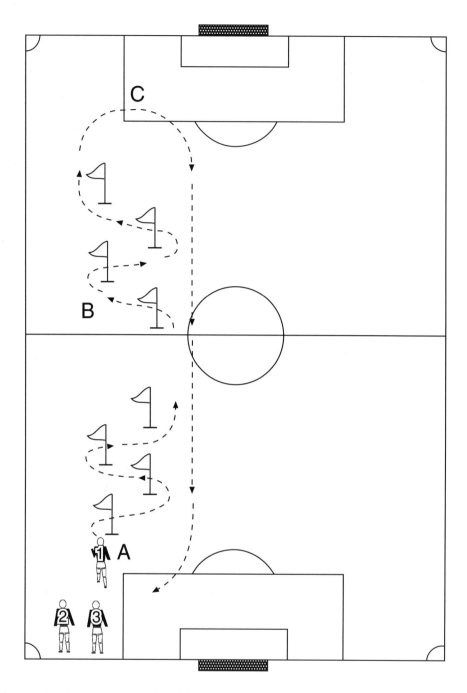

Diagram 19. Interval training: Dribble run.

four, three players recover while one is working: a recovery to work ratio of 3:1. A group of two produces a recovery to work ratio of 1:1.

(a) Obstacle Dribbling. Diagram 19

On a signal, the first player dribbles from A, through the obstacle course at B, to C where he turns. He returns to A at top sprinting speed .

2 takes over when, having entered the penalty area, 1 passes the ball to him.

Players may be required to use a specific dribbling method, e.g. one foot only; or with the outside of each foot; or using each foot alternately, playing the ball in the air and so on.

On completion of a run a player, alone or with other recovering players, practices specific soccer skills. The player's pulse rate should be at or about 150 beats per minute after two or three reps. rising to 180 b.p.m. after 8+/- and dropping to about 130 b.p.m. during the recovery phases.

(b) Team triple relays.

The players start as in the diagram 19 and are always diagonally across the course from each other. The players run outside the pitch. The 'course' can accommodate twelve or more players; here there are 12.

All players must:
- run and dribble a ball.
- dribble in and out of the two cones.
- give and receive a return pass at each of the changeover stations.
- finish where they start.

The team run is completed and timing stops when the last player is back in his original starting position.

(c) Weave runs.

These are suitable for a relatively large group of players training together since three players run at the same time. e.g. If nine players (3 x 3) are in one training group, three work while six recover.

In **Diagram 20** players A, B,and C run from within one penalty area to the other and return to their starting area. Starting with B in the center they pass to each other in turn, follow their own pass to run outside the player to whom they pass. Between each penalty area each player must receive and pass the ball at least four times. A full size pitch can take any number of three player groups. In the diagram, 18 players are split into three groups with two threes in each group. Each group therefore is working on a work: recovery ratio of 1:1.

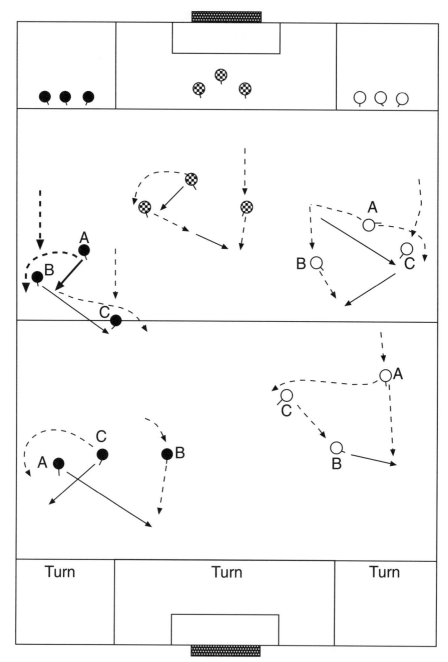

Diagram 20. Three player weave runs.

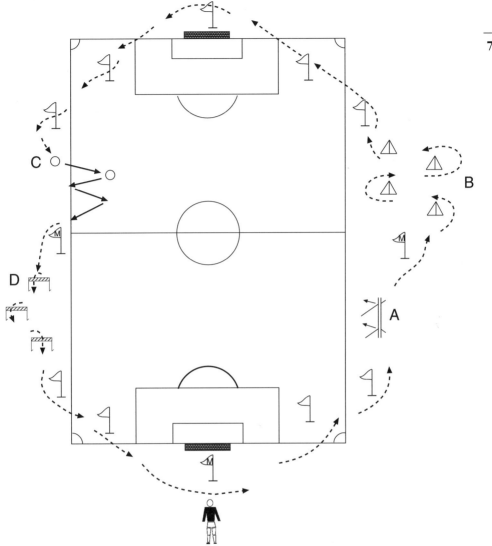

Diagram 21. 'D' Runs.

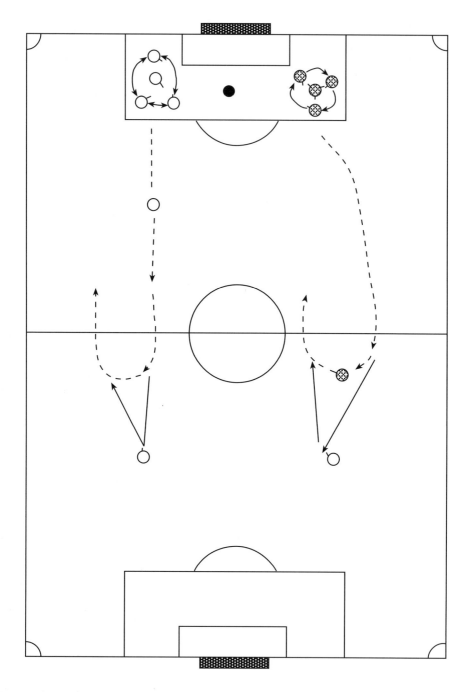

Diagram 22. Speed: Stamina Work.

Duration running. ('D' runs)

General stamina may be improved by runs of fixed duration where the players try to progressively increase the distance covered. The duration recommended is between 10 and 15 minutes.

In the following 'D' run, players follow the course set out in Diagram 21.
- All running is done with a ball.
- Distance is calculated in laps of the course plus so many quarters. Markers indicate the quarter laps.
- Players commence their 'D' runs from a particular marker and work out their finishing distance in laps to the nearest quarter from it.
- At each 'skill station' they must complete the ball exercises set down. Players try to increase the distance covered in a standard time.
- The quicker they negotiate the 'skill station' the sooner they can run to extend the distance covered.
- The suggested course will accommodate 16 players comfortably.
- Times are set and distances measured as precisely as possible and recorded.

7.42 SPEED: Stamina

Here speed is the primary and stamina the secondary objective.

Speed is gained from quality runs rather than quantity ; the speed attained is over-ridingly important. Between each high quality sprint a player is allowed to recover substantially. The amount of work done must not inhibit players from attaining the highest possible speeds when required.

Training activities.

(a) Diagram 22. Players work in large groups, six or seven or more, giving work to recovery ratios of 1:5, 1:6 or greater thereby allowing considerable recovery to take place.
- For the 10-15 runs, (diagram 22) players sprint flat out.
- Recovering players play 'keep ball' games, 2 v 3 or 2 v 4. This activity caters for the required stamina element.
- For motivation, time standards and team records are set for runs of different repetition distances.

Each player must be timed over a single speed run every month say. If his speed doesn't increase he is not training at optimum speed or the sprint course needs adjusting to allow for higher speed.

Players may fool coaches for some of the time but they won't fool the stop-watch for any of it.

(b) Weaves. (Diagram 20)

Players work in teams of six threes. Three groups at each end of the course.

A run is from penalty area to penalty area. Each group completes 10 to 15 runs. Each player in a threesome must touch the ball at least twice during one repetition. A changeover takes place only when all three incoming players are inside the penalty area.

When not involved in a run or when waiting to be the next running group, recovering players play 4 v 2 or 2 v 1 'keep ball' behind each goal or in the penalty areas. Each running group must complete at least two 'weaves' between the start and finish of a run. See Diagram 20, following the completion, of which they all head for home as fast as possible, one of them dribbling the ball. All runs are at top speed. During a run the ball should be played 'generously' in front of each receiving player to enable him to maintain top speed: too far and the group will not complete the required two weaves: too close and there will be an inadequate speed element in the performance.

(c) Shuttle Sprints. (Diagram 23)

The player passes or receives as he passes a marker. The course is 40 to 50 yards long and the training group numbers 6 to 8 players

Regular, weekly interval training, with occasional duration runs, twice a month say, is likely to produce the best soccer stamina-speed mixes.

7.43 AGILITY Training.

Agility involves changes of position over short distances or changes of body shape (as in goalkeeping or similar soccer activity), at optimum speed.

Agility training by definition involves the element of speed but it may have stamina as a subsidiary objective, for example when heavy playing pitches are imminent. Where agility is the primary objective, the quality of each run is the important consideration.

Training activities.

(a) A course is set out as in Diagram 24. Player A runs to receive the ball beyond each marker which is 5 - 10 meters from the start. After carrying out the set skill beyond each marker, the player returns to the starting mark.

Serving players are stationed five meters beyond each marker.

At S1 the player controls a chest high service and with his second touch returns the ball to the server on the ground.

At S2. the player jumps high to head the ball back to the server.

At S3. the player volleys a return pass .

Each player works and then takes the place of a server who replaces him. Skill accuracy at high speed is vital. After the three players have run, they practice soccer techniques together or individually thereby recovering actively. The sequence is begun and increased to accommodate current and future fitness levels.

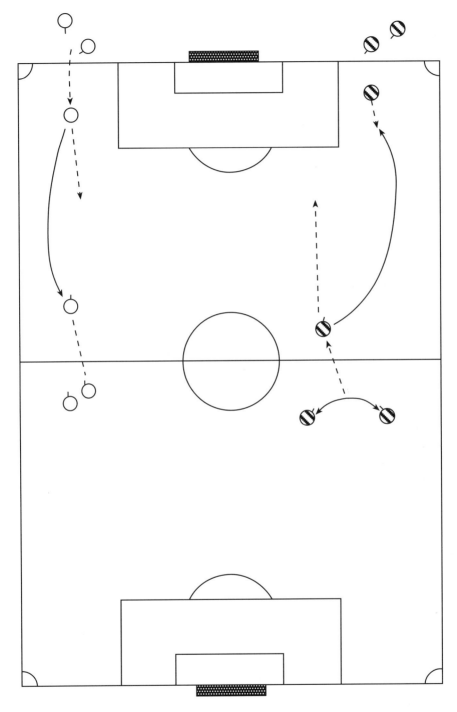

Diagram 23. Shuttle Sprints.

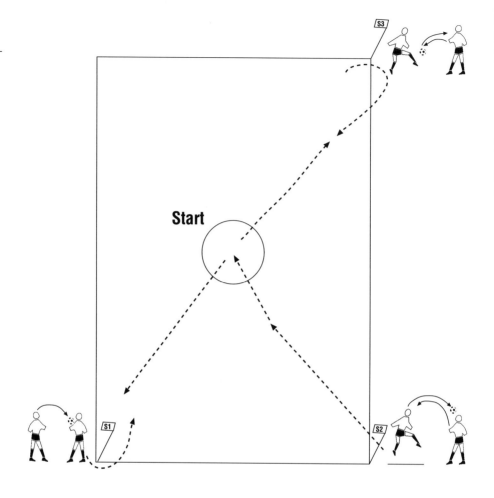

Diagram 24. Agility Course.

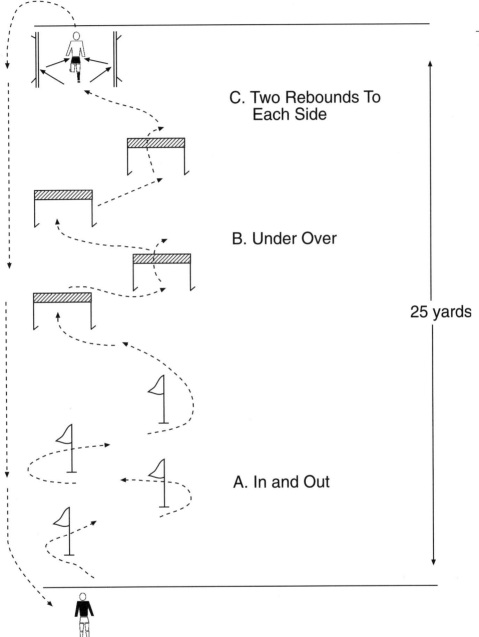

C. Two Rebounds To
   Each Side

B. Under Over

25 yards

A. In and Out

Diagram 25.

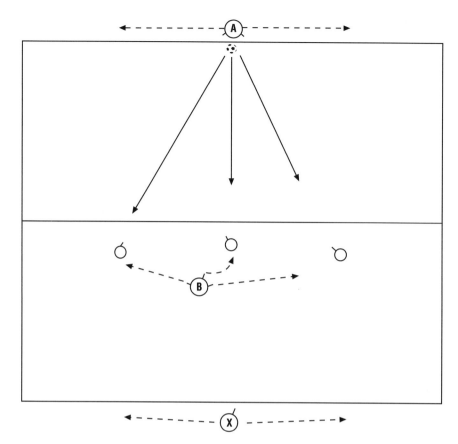

Diagram 26.

(b.) The course is 25 meters long making a total 'run' of 50 meters.
Outwards, players negotiate the obstacles set out as in diagram 25 playing a ball through, round or over an obstacle as indicated. The return run is completed at optimum speed while dribbling. The run is completed when the ball is returned to its starting circle.

7.44 AGILITY: Stamina.

Using the same agility circuit as previously, the training emphasis can be switched to stamina by increasing the number of service stations to five and by reducing the number of working players. ie. by increasing the work to recovery ratio.

Training activities
(a) S1, S2, S3 are the same, at S4 the player receives a ground pass and dribbles round the marker before returning the ball to the server.
• At S5 the player receives the ball in the air, controls it and inter-passes with the server five times before completing his run.

• Each player, in turn, should complete 10 to 20 runs.

• If the required heart rate effect (180 b.p.m.) is not achieved soon enough the number of players working should be reduced to three or even to two. This means that the servers only act as servers.

• A player is timed for each run.

(b) In diagram 26 three receivers are positioned across the twenty yard box. A server is twenty yards in front of the receivers. Player B may station himself anywhere behind the receivers. The server passes to one of the receivers who controls the pass and turns to pass to target player X. Player B moves to prevent the receiver turning to pass. If he is successful the receiver must return the pass to the server who then passes to another receiver. B moves from receiver to receiver to prevent passes being made to the target player behind him.

• The working player receives 10 - 15 repetitions.

In all training programs, team records or standards - excellent, very good, average, not so good and poor - should be established and shown.

Setting standards and achieving records are vital to effective training; they motivate players (and coaches) and provide invaluable indications of training effectiveness. . . or otherwise!

7.45 Strength (Power).

All sports training should be based on sound, all-round physical development. Soccer makes demands on all parts of the body, often under the most demanding playing conditions. As tiredness encroaches, those aspects of the neuro-muscular system least prepared will be the first to let the player down.

The application of strength at speed is important in most team sports. In soccer, without leg power long passing and distance shooting are unlikely. Without leg power, an explosive start to a decisive sprint will not happen. Without dynamic thrust, a goalkeeper or a striker, competing to contact the same high cross will not quite get there. . . at least not soon enough!

Training activities.

Leg power can be developed by playing small-sided games on narrow pitches which have significant slopes end to end.

(a) The players play 8 v 8 on an area 100 yards long and 50 yards wide.
The pitch has a steep slope end to end. The game has two 'conditions':

• a shot cannot be taken by the team playing uphill until all its players are in the forward half of the pitch.

• the uphill team cannot move the ball out of its defending half until all its players are in it.

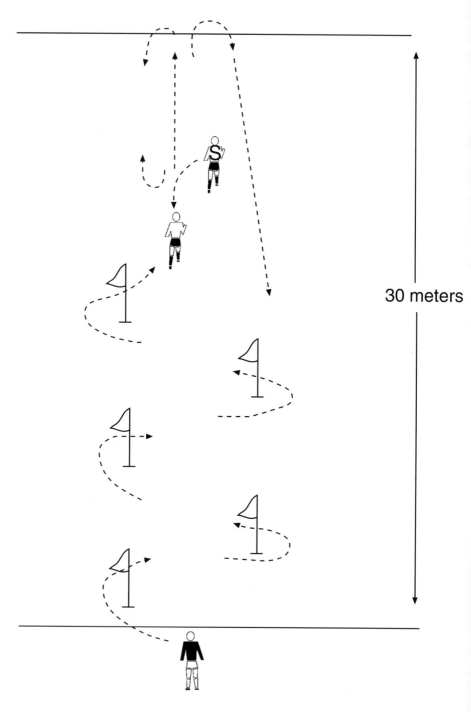

30 meters

Diagram 27. Uphill slalom.

Other 'conditions' might be:
- on receiving the ball an uphill player must run the ball at and past an opponent before passing.
- uphill players are allowed only two sideways or back passes before someone must run the ball uphill towards the opposing goal.

These 'conditions' ensure that the 'uphill team' must work hard against the resistance of the slope. The slope angle is much more important than the quality of the playing surface. In any case soccer skills and 'touch' are best developed on rough, unpredictable practice surfaces.

Practice upon muddy, 'heavy' ground, on soft sand, against strong wind or in thick, long grass develop power. It is important for players to experience adverse weather and ground conditions. Too many professional teams are quick to transfer training and practice indoors where conditions and surfaces bear little relationship to the actual playing environment. Weak, unimaginative coaches make those sort of decisions. . . often influenced by player power!

(b) Uphill Slalom.

The course on a steep slope (diagram 27) is 30 meters long. The players dribble the ball in and out of the cones. After leaving the last cone the ball is played to the waiting server who picks it up and serves a fairly high ball for the dribbling player to head back to him. The dribbler returns to the last cone before returning to receive a second serve to head.

After the second header the player dribbles from the 20 metre marker to the end and back again three times. He then returns to the starting point as fast as he can.

Players requiring out of the ordinary jumping power, goalkeepers for example, can wear vests with pockets in which weights are inserted to provide extra resistance. Weighted boots allow players to practice skills against resistance.

A drag weight, e.g. a car tire, attached to a player by a harness and pulled behind him while dribbling, for example, will increase leg power. Soft sand training for goalkeepers and for other players who need to increase their jumping power is very effective. The reduced resistance to thrust at take-off makes players develop greater speed of muscular contraction to achieve required height. Contraction speed thus developed will lead to significantly improved height off firmer surfaces. All practices in sand can be based upon relevant soccer techniques thereby ensuring optimum transfer of training effects into match performance.

Muscular power developed through weight training is transferable but obviously the limb movements are not those of the soccer player. Weight training effects transfer less effectively than activities derived from the game itself.

7.46 Suppleness.

The older the player the more important the maintenance of good ranges of movement in all joints and 'hinges'. High degrees of suppleness, ie. flexibility (bendability) and extensibility (stretchability), are natural to most children. Movement ranges become limited when joints and the tendons and muscles which move them are used less frequently if at all. Use them or lose them.

The more we limit movement in our joints, the greater the likelihood of strain or rupture when we do need the full range. Soccer players never know when they will need highly unusual limb and body positions. They (and all of us) need to practice joint mobilizing activities from an early age and continue them for as long as possible, which really means forever.

It is hardly possible to design game-based exercises which will increase suppleness. The following activities will maintain existing suppleness in the major joint complexes. They will increase it where the exercise is taken into its 'end' position and a little further, periodically. The 'end' position is where a joint can be taken no further by normal activity.

All supplying work must be done slowly. Swinging exercises and exercises done to a rhythm in which the limbs and the body are encouraged to develop momentum are dangerous.

Training Activities.
(a) Neck - slow head circling using the tip of the chin to describe as big a circle as possible. Circle 5 - 10 times in each direction.
• stretch the head backwards to reach as far down the spine as possible. Bend the head forward to reach as far down the chest with the chin as possible. In each case hold the 'end' position to a count of 5 seconds. Repeat each stretch and bend 5 - 10 times.

(b) Arms and shoulders - full arm stretch circling backwards so that the upper arms brush the ears as they pass them.
• following 5 circles hold the arms at full stretch overhead, with the upper arms brushing the head. Press the stretched arms as far backwards as possible and hold for a count of 5 seconds. Relax, shake the arms loose and repeat.

(c) Upper spine
(1) standing left foot forward, twist the trunk as far as possible to the left, press to the left 5 times then hold the furthest twist position for a count of 5 seconds. Repeat the sequence with the right foot forward and twisting to the right.
(2) prone lying, hands underneath the shoulders, press the upper body as far backwards as possible and hold the end position for a count of 5 seconds.
(3) standing and remaining upright, force the chin to move down the chest to the furthest possible position.

(d) Lower spine
(1) kneel sitting, twist the spine to the right as far as possible, hold the end

position for a count of 5 seconds. Repeat to the left and so on.

(2) back lying, feet flat on the ground, hands beneath the shoulders, push up into the 'crab' position until the knees are straight. Hold that position for a count of 5 seconds and repeat.

(3) long sitting, slide the hands as far down the legs as possible to reach the toes or beyond. Hold the end position hold it for the count of 5.

(e) Hips

(1) wide astride standing, knees straight, lower both elbows to touch the ground between the feet and then alternately to touch each foot.

(2) forward astride standing, hands on hips, press the hips as close to the ground as possible keeping the back leg as straight as possible. Find the end position and hold it for 5.

(3) hurdle sitting, reach for the front foot with the opposite hand pressing the chest as close to the front thigh as possible. Hold the end position for 5. Change legs.

(f) Ankles

(1) long sitting, alternate ankle circling, 5 clockwise and 5 anti-clockwise.

(2) long sitting, ankles together, stretch both sets of toes towards the ground, keeping the knees straight. Find the end position and hold it for the count of five.

(3) running on the spot, keeping both feet in contact with the ground, as each knee lifts stretch that ankle to point towards the ground.

7.5 Age Related Training.

Different stages of development require different training emphases. Young children may react unfavorably to any emphasis on endurance preferring to run fast for short periods rather than moderately fast for long. Similarly young soccer players, at certain stages of development, may reject repetitive technical practice preferring to practice through play. They are not being difficult; their development 'timers' govern their attitudes. This may seem inconvenient to their teacher or coach but information from these natural timers should never be ignored.

Chapter 8
Fitness Testing

Fitness for soccer players is an often misunderstood concept. Significant demands are made in the game upon players' speed and agility, strength and power, stamina and suppleness and not least upon the highly precise use of skill. Great strides have been made in creating a scientific sub culture in the world of sports training particularly, but not exclusively, in those events measurable in terms of 'how fast', 'how far' and 'how high'. Performance requirements for those events are to a great extent quantifiable, albeit not totally.

Measurement of the quality of will needed to produce almost unbelievable effort in certain circumstances is, as yet, beyond sports scientists.

In soccer, which in itself is not quantifiable, other than crudely and with hindsight, fitness testing has been based upon work done with track and field athletes and participants in similar sports. Performance in soccer has been divided and sectioned off into supposedly testable areas and the whole, such as it is, reassembled in the hope that test results might have high diagnostic and thereby prognostic value. If only the affairs of man were that simple.

We simply do not know, nor can we predict, just how much work a player will be required to do, or will choose to do, during any particular match.

Nevertheless it is important that player preparation (practice and training) which is planned to be progressive should be evaluated on some sort of standardized basis. Even if a coach makes subjective assessment, he can standardize his assessments to some extent by checking off player performances against a list of the characteristics which form the basis of his judgments.

There are coaches and talent scouts who claim to 'have an eye' for a good player. Some of those with whom I discussed this and related skill assessment problems do indeed have mental lists of performance characteristics against which they score a player's performance. When I suggested that they wrote down those lists of characteristics upon which they might make recruitment recommendations, they were strangely reluctant to do so. They would talk about performance criteria but preferred to keep secret the ultra-precious aspects of their personal insights and knowledge. The value and exclusivity of those insights were, I am sure, more imaginary than real.

I have stated repeatedly that almost all aspects of player preparation can be done efficiently and effectively within the contexts of game skills or individual technical skills. I make no apology for repeating that, in my judgment, the greater a player's (and a team's) skill, the less the work they need to do to win matches. Having said that, I am sufficiently a realist to know that, occasionally, skills (team and individual) are inexplicably fallible and that to win matches in which fallibility occurs, teams need ten percent extra in the way of physiological and/or psychological capability. The tests which are recommended here are useful for individual players to compare their own performances before, during and after training cycles lasting for four weeks or more. They have no value if used to compare the performances of one player against those of others. There are no absolutes worth the name in soccer preparation.

Finally, when administering tests it is important that all test conditions are rigorously standardized.

Power Tests:

(a) Standing Long Jump.
- A reasonable test of leg power is the standing long jump.
- A player should be introduced to the standing long jump, initially, as a skill.
- He should be taught and allowed to practice those aspects. . . arm swinging, knee bending and stretching before take off, double leg 'shoot' and so on. . . which contribute to improved performances.
- The test itself can become the training regime. In it, a player may train wearing heavier than normal clothing or footwear. On test he should revert to standardized test clothing.

(b) Vertical Jump.
The player stands sideways to a wall. Keeping both feet flat on the ground and using his inside arm, he reaches up to touch the wall as high as he can. His fingers dipped in powdered chalk will make a mark. He is allowed to find the best of three stretches. Then, jumping off two feet, he makes another mark as high as he can above his first mark. The difference between the two marks is his vertical jump index. Again, any practice wearing heavier clothing or jumping off a softer surface will build up power.

Power: Speed Tests.

(a) Double Foot Jumps.
- Four hurdles, 2 feet six inches in height, are set out 2 feet apart. Players use a succession of four double foot jumps to complete the course; they are timed from the first take off to the final touch down.

(b) The course is 20 yards long as in diagram 28.
- At A. an obstacle 2 feet six inches high is positioned.
- From the start, the player runs to the obstacle at A and jumps over it three times using a double foot jump to do so.
- He then hops on the foot of his choice to the turn at B.
- From B, having touched the ground beyond the turn mark, he runs back to repeat the three double foot jumps at A.
- From the obstacle he runs back to the start line.

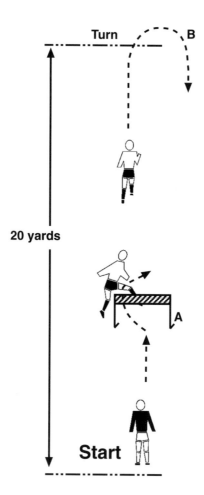

Turn B

20 yards

A

Start

Diagram 28.

Speed Tests.

The player uses a running start to pass through a starting gate and sprints all out through another gate forty yards away. The gates are angled towards the time keeper. This enables one time keeper to judge the start and finish.

Speed: Agility Tests.

(a) Weave Run.

• The course, as in diagram 29 is thirty feet long and players run there and back to complete one run. Their running pattern must be as in the diagram. The first hurdle is 12 feet from the start line. The second and subsequent hurdles are 6 feet apart. The fourth hurdle is also the turning point for the run.

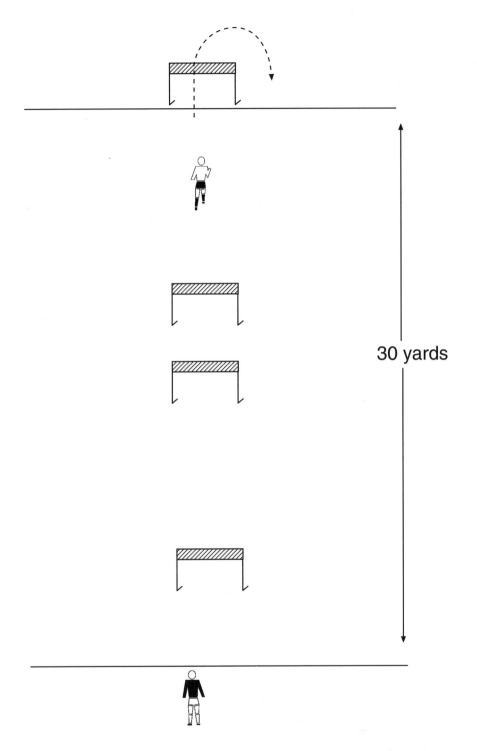

30 yards

Diagram 29. Speed test - Steeple chase.

(b) Tip and Run.

- The course is as in the diagram 29
- Ball A is on a mark 5 yards from the center of the start line.
- Ball B is 10 yards from the center of the start line and,
- Ball C is 15 yards from the same point. From the start line a player runs to A, tips it away from its mark and returns to touch down behind any part of the start line with any part of his body.
- He repeats the run, tip and return to each of the balls B and C finishing over the start line.
- A successful 'tip' is any movement of a ball, however slight, off its spot.
- The course is 60 yards long in total.

General Stamina (cr) Tests.

A reasonable endurance quotient can be established by first timing a player for a 200 yard sprint. After full rest he is timed for a 60 yard sprint. The endurance quotient is found by dividing the 200 yard time by the 60 yard time.

Alternatively, cr capability may be tested by a timed run over 300 yards. The 300 yards may be a track based course, a 3 x 100 yards straight course or a shuttle run with each leg of the shuttle 60 yards long where the player will finish at the opposite end to where he started.

Local Stamina (cv) Tests.
Shuttle Runs

- Four balls are 3 yds., 6 yds., 9 yds., and 12 yds from the start line respectively.
- The player runs to each ball in turn dribbling it back to the start line until the four balls are behind the start line.
- The player then rests for a timed period of 30 seconds.
- The second run involves dribbling each ball in turn out to its original marker. On completion of a full run, the player again rests for 30 seconds.
- The test requires the completion of a set number of runs to suit the training condition of each player. Times and progress are recorded.

Whenever possible soccer training activities, with or without the ball, should be the basis of training tests if not the actual tests themselves.

The need is for reasonable standardization of the training activities and the circumstances in which they take place. It's not much use training and practicing on the hard floor of a sports hall and trying to test certain qualities on, say, a grass surface. Similarly the difference between the same grass surface when very wet and when dry would invalidate any attempt to draw fitness conclusions from any sort of test activity.

In soccer, tests are useful motivational devices and useful indicators but not too much should be claimed for their scientific value.